TOCQUEVILLE
AND THE
NATURE OF DEMOCRACY

TOCQUEVILLE
AND THE
NATURE OF DEMOCRACY

Pierre Manent
Translated by
John Waggoner
Foreword by
Harvey C. Mansfield

Rowman & Littlefield Publishers, Inc.

ROWMAN & LITTLEFIELD PUBLISHERS, INC.

Published in the United States of America
by Rowman & Littlefield Publishers, Inc.
4720 Boston Way, Lanham, Maryland 20706

3 Henrietta Street
London WC2E 8LU, England

British Cataloging in Publication Information Available

Library of Congress Cataloging-in-Publication Data

Manent, Pierre,
[Tocqueville et la nature de la démocratie. English]
Tocqueville and the nature of democracy / by Pierre Manent ; translated by
John Waggoner.
p.   cm.
Includes bibliographical references.
1. Tocqueville, Alexis de, 1805–1859. 2. Democracy.   I. Title.
JC229.T8M3213 1996   320'.092—dc20   95-38604 CIP

ISBN 0-8476-8115-7 (cloth: alk. paper)
ISBN 0-8476-8116-5 (pbk.: alk. paper)

Printed in the United States of America

⊗™The paper used in this publication meets the minimum requirements of
American National Standard for Information Sciences—Permanence of
Paper for Printed Library Materials, ANSI Z39.48-1984.

CONTENTS

FOREWORD

Pierre Manent's elegant and profound work is the best introduction I know to the greatness of Tocqueville. It is one
among a number of books on Tocqueville recently published in
France that attempt to recover for present use an author who
had been sadly neglected by his countrymen. Since World War
Two French thought had been in a near-universal subjection to
Marxism—with the proud exception of Raymond Aron—while
being frequently dazzled by emanations, such as the existen-
tialism of Jean-Paul Sartre and the structuralism of Michel
Foucault, from the powerful mind of Martin Heidegger. But for
two decades now, thanks to the influence of Alexander Solzhen-
itsyn, the new anti-Marxist historiography of the French Revolution led by François Furet, and, simply and finally, the collapse of communism and socialism, French philosophers and
intellectuals have liberated themselves not only from Marxism
but also from the varieties of neo-Marxism that had taken
nourishment from Heidegger. Liberalism returned to Paris, of
all places—at once the most and the least bourgeois city in the
world. The French wisely turned to historical liberalism, to the
nineteenth-century liberalism of Benjamin Constant, François
Guizot, and Alexis de Tocqueville (which is, they realized, their
own), as well as to the English liberals and the American
Founders. For some reason they did not take to the more
overtly theoretical or analytical liberalism of Anglo-American
philosophers today.

Pierre Manent's book is of such quality that it resists being placed in its time. But it offers a compelling contrast to the theories widely available in Anglo-America that issue in moral demands made on politics from outside politics. Such theories overlook the requirements of politics itself, which may have its own demands to be made on morality; and they willfully ignore the nature of man, which may also be both contrary and favorable to morality. Manent, following Tocqueville, begins from the regime, the modern political regime *par excellence*, that is democracy, and in accord with the title of his book, *Tocqueville and the Nature of Democracy*, he immediately raises the question of the naturalness of democracy.

Why is democracy so pervasive and democratization so irresistible? Any doubt that democracy was everywhere or that it had spread into every part of society would have to be raised from a democratic point of view—because we wanted more democracy than we have or can see. At the outset Tocqueville calls the progress of democracy a "providential fact," but of course he goes far beyond this judgment (though without canceling it) to show what is intrinsic to democracy, enabling it to advance and succeed. Democracy is not some frail flower that God wished to protect against hostile circumstances. Manent presents an analysis that unveils the nature of democracy by stages carefully set forth in his chapters. His analysis is attentive to Tocqueville's text, but what Tocqueville presents rhetorically and with all the evidence of his wonderful observations Manent condenses in an argument of political philosophy.

Tocqueville's fundamental observation is the equality of conditions in modern society. No hierarchy of conventional superiorities can be found there such as used to exist not only in traditional aristocracies but even in the ancient democracies. Equality of conditions proceeds from democracy as a political regime, but it also engenders, or reflects—cause and effect become confused—a democratic society or "social state" separate from or even prior to politics. Democracy produces a sense of independence in its citizens, a sentiment that each is a whole because he depends on no one else; and the democratic dogma states that every citizen is competent to govern his own life. Hence democracy is not merely, perhaps not primarily, a form of government; or it is form of government that almost denies the need for government. And as a society, democracy is anti-social; it severs individuals from one another by pronouncing each of them equally free. All the traditional relationships are broken or weakened, and democratic politics has to take on the task of reuniting what the democratic social state has taken apart. This is Tocqueville's famous art or science of association.

By stripping individual men of their conventional relation-ships democracy appears to be more natural than its counter-part, aristocracy. Democracy treats men as they are, whereas aristocracy deforms them in relationships they would never have entered into except by the powerful influence of customs and institutions, which force them to be more superior and more inferior to one another than they naturally are. Yet, true as this main point remains, it is not the whole truth. Manent shows in his most important chapter, the seventh, on democracy and the nature of man, that democracy has its conventions working in accordance with its nature, and that aristocracy, too, has a natural basis—in the natural inequalities of man. Democracy, it appears, has the advantage of the naturally stronger force of human equality; for is not our nature principally the universal nature we have equally? Thus democracy can afford to be mild, representing as it does our commonality, our mutual recognition, even our sympathy with one another. But aristocracy must be harsh in order to sustain the inequalities that are hard to see and belong to a few and so are naturally weak.

Thus, as all modern peoples have seen and felt, democracy is more naturally just than aristocracy. But its very mildness, its ready accessibility to our passions and attachments, brings with it problems peculiar to our time. By being so attractive, democracy is not sufficiently demanding: it depends on religion, which glorifies man's mission in life, but tends to produce a uniform pantheism that degrades him; it needs the political freedom that calls for sacrifice on great occasions, but routinely operates on "self-interest well understood"; and it yearns for greatness while distrusting the great and without having the means or discipline for greatness on its own. Above all, democracy does not know where it tends and where it should go. It empowers us all, and at the same time, through the democratic dogma of individual competence, it renders us complacent and easily satisfied with the mediocre.

Thanks to the marvelous immediacy of Tocqueville's work, Manent's analysis is a meditation on our democracy today; and with the aid of Tocqueville's equally wonderful detachment, Manent compels us to think about our nature. The relevance and the permanence are together in this showpiece of political philosophy.

Harvey C. Mansfield

Cambridge, Massachusetts, October 1995

PREFACE TO THE 1993 FRENCH EDITION

The book that you have before you has its source in the thought of Tocqueville or, in any case, in several of its principal themes. It was written at a time when the thought of Tocqueville was undergoing a process of rediscovery—or rather, discovery—by recent political thinkers in my country. It does not claim to offer a full disquisition on the thought of the French thinker,[1] but only to highlight what is most original in his interpretation of our political destiny. It is here that numerous misunderstandings arise. Most can be traced to one simple fact. No one seriously believes that an author, dead for more than a century, can say anything to us about the novelties that we face, that he can explain us to ourselves. This is precisely what Tocqueville accomplishes, it seems to me, when he elaborates the idea of democracy. Understanding of his elaboration can only be had through an effort on our part to understand ourselves. It would thus please me to think that the republication of this work would bring to the reader a sense not only of the difficulty of my research but also, I hope, certain of its fruits.

Nothing is more tempting than to regard the democratic regime that we know as natural for the human species. This is what we all spontaneously do, partly because habit has made it "ours," but also because we have the vague but strong feeling that the whole of historic experience in Europe, or the West, leads toward it, that the destiny of others is to join us in partaking of its benefits. These feelings are not foreign to Tocqueville. He was even one of the first to formulate them, and he did so in an impressive fashion. But democracy is also quite another thing: something that happens to us, that transforms us, that changes the depths as well as the surface of our lives, something that we do not desire because we do not take cognizance of it when it is most at work, when it has transformed us the most. On the one hand, democracy is the regime most intrinsic to human nature when it is finally free to express its wishes, but democracy is also something that happens to human nature without its knowing or really wanting what happens. The greatness of Tocqueville was his capacity at one and the same time for promoting the clear hope that democracy entails while deepening a sense for its doleful secret.

The democracy in question, our democracy, is not just one political regime among others. It is not, like ancient democracy, one category in a general classification of political regimes, constituting one of the legitimate forms of human cohabitation, a form that is eternally possible and eternally susceptible to degeneration and replacement by another. Modern democracy breaks with this natural cycle. It succeeds other political regimes, all others, and sweeps them forward irresistibly and definitely. From the moment democracy appears, the historic landscape is utterly transformed. Political regimes that seemed most different now seem to resemble each other. Compared to modern democracy, ancient democracy and the *ancien régime* of France, for example, equally belong to "aristocracy," Tocqueville tells us. Thus, there appears one world, modern democracy, separated from the other, ancient, world in all its manifest forms, all the ancient worlds taken together. They are, Tocqueville tells us, "like two distinct humanities."

Such a sentiment is not unique to Tocqueville. Marx and Nietzsche, for example, share it. The sentiment of the nineteenth century boils down to a sense that something heretofore unexpressed and unheard of was under way. It was to conceptualize this extraordinary novelty that the great intellectual systems characteristic of the century were elaborated, the philosophies of history. Comte and Marx had the conviction of henceforth knowing the direction of historic becoming leading to the New, while Nietzsche affirmed the preeminently arbitrary character of each historic creation, and therefore also modern democracy, as the expression and effect of a vulgar will. Tocqueville does not make claim to such sublime views. He clearly thinks that democratic developments indicate the direction of history, but concerns himself with the precise meaning of this general proposition. To understand exactly means, first and foremost, to describe exactly.

What Tocqueville describes is the transformation of man by democracy. It is a new human type: democratic man. He is not characterized by particular ends. He is not distinguished from "aristocratic" man as, for example, the monk is distinguished from the warrior, or the generous person from the avaricious one. He does not look to fulfill an end, but to put into operation a certain hypothesis, according to which all men are born and live free and equal in certain rights, with the consequence that there is no legitimate obedience except that to which one has previously consented. Instead of declaiming against the "bourgeois," like Rousseau or Marx, or the "last man," like Nietzsche, Tocqueville analyzes with extraordinary penetration how human life in all its aspects is turned upside down by this hypothesis. In the pages that follow, I have tried to restore his analysis. As to its validity, the validity of this description of democratic man, each reader who observes others and observes himself must evaluate it himself and for himself. No "science of society" can dispense with this intellectual effort. Or rather, no true science of society can exist without such an evaluation.

Tocqueville underscores the fact that democratic man is governed by the dogma of the sovereignty of the people over his individual actions. This dogma is silent on the content or the ends of these actions. The rights of man are deliberately silent on the ends of man. The more that man considers himself as a being who possesses rights, the more the guarantee of these rights progresses, the more the question of ends is pushed back, and the silence becomes deafening. But just who affirms himself thus? What is man? Tocqueville is one of the very few authors who helps us face this question, the only question, in the final analysis, that must interest us.

Paris, January, 1993

INTRODUCTION

"This book follows no one's lead, strictly. In writing it, I did not intend to serve or oppose any party. I have endeavored to see things, not differently, but further than the parties," Alexis de Tocqueville wrote in the *Introduction*[1] to the first volume of *Democracy in America*. This is how he defined the task of political education that he took upon himself in offering to his contemporaries the analysis that was the fruit of his reflections during a trip to the United States from May 1831 to February 1832. To begin with, this traveler is a French citizen who, in the juncture between the Restoration and the beginning of the July Monarchy, sees his country torn between parties. Some of them dread and others hope for the continuation of the advance of democracy that, according to a famous expression of the period, was "at the point of overflowing its banks."

It is not so much that some are wrong to fear and others to hope; it is that their fears and hopes are not well directed. Tocqueville goes to America to discover exactly what one has to fear and what one is allowed to hope for from democracy.[2]

If this citizen is without partisan passions, if on the contrary, he wants to correct the vision of each of the parties, he is still in the grip of one violent passion. This democratic revolution that "is at the point of overflowing its banks," that has in France just uprooted the most glorious of European aristocracies, inspires in him "a sort of religious terror."[3] Considering the history of Christian Europe as a whole, he sees the "equality of conditions" progress from century to century, with all indications showing it to be an irreversible, even providential, movement. The gradual development of the equality of conditions is therefore a providential fact because it possesses the principal characteristics of Providence: it is universal, lasting, and always escapes the power of human control.[4] Therefore, any pretensions to stop it would be ridiculous, bound to fail, perhaps impious.[5] The only reasonable step to take—imposed upon us by the pressure of events themselves—is to come to an accurate conception of the end of this process that it would be vain to try to hinder and premature, in France, to judge.

This "gradual development of the equality of conditions" is concurrent with the abolition of the aristocratic order, more than half prepared by the kings,[6] and brought to completion by the French Revolution. The features of the new society are, in France, difficult to make out, because the dust of battle has not yet settled, and the passions stimulated by the combat disturb our vision. Now, "there is one country in the world where the great social revolution I am talking about seems to have just about reached its natural limits. It has worked itself out in a simple and easy manner, or rather, one can say that this country sees the results of the democratic revolution that is working itself out among us, without having a revolution itself."[7] Tocqueville will look to America for a clear and tranquil view of this democracy whose history in Europe, in France in particular, offers only a confused and violent advance. He will therefore look for the veritable end of the process in which Europe remains immersed.

Tocqueville is a voyager in quest of an essence, a nature—that of democracy.[8] His quest is an effort to overcome by intellectual clarity "the religious terror" he feels. By understanding the nature of democracy, he will know what he can hope for and what he must fear.

The first two chapters of *Democracy in America* are the record of his marveling. The advantages of a serene America are contrasted with a convulsive Europe, beginning with nature itself.[9] It is as if North America had been readied by God to be the theater of a grand human enterprise.[10] This magnificent land was, in a sense, empty before the arrival of the Europeans. "The Indians occupied it but did not possess it." It is by agriculture that man appropriated the land. Providence, in placing the Europeans in the midst of the riches of the New World, seems to have given them a short-term *usufruct*. The riches were there, in a certain sense, only *waiting for them*.[11] Providence, in America, does not inspire terror.

The human enterprise for which Providence has prepared such a promising background is itself also marked by signs of divine favor.[12] It is unique in history that we know how a republic like America was founded. Better yet, its founders knew what they were doing. They belonged to the leisured and enlightened classes of the English mother country. As a group, they were relatively the most enlightened ever encountered in history. They were in no way constrained by necessity, but obeyed an "intellectual need." They "wanted to cause an idea to triumph."[13] Thus, "democracy, such as Antiquity never dared to dream, emerged fully grown and armed from the midst of the old feudal society."[14] The Puritans had engaged in a process of abstraction, of selection, then of the transplantation of the democratic idea.[15] What is thus under investigation by Tocqueville is a political experiment conducted by individuals who were particularly enterprising, competent, and talented, who acted in full consciousness of what they were doing.

From the pole of Europe and the obscure and irresistible process that is transforming it, we suddenly move to the opposite extreme, a pole characterized by a clear idea, a founding that demonstrates human freedom and control and that can be distinctly dated. The only history that remains for the American Republic is its spatial expansion. To Europe belongs the Providence that elicits terror and is marked by obscurity and a necessary process, the trace of whose origins is lost. To America belongs a generous and maternal Providence, marked by a clear idea and a free and intelligent founding. What marks European history is inverted in America. One can in America, even find a pitiable and derisory version of aristocracy, so awesome and so glorious in Europe. These are the Indians[16] that one does not conquer like men, but chases before oneself like some kind of animal, so vulnerable are they as a consequence of their "savage virtues."[17]

Tocqueville tells us that Chapter Two, devoted to the starting point of the Americans, gives us the key to "almost the whole work."[18] Thus, the key to American democracy is found in the characteristics that distinguish America from Europe. Yet it is in this America that Tocqueville will look for "an image of democracy itself."

These differences, as considerable as they are and because they are so considerable, serve only to highlight *the very thing* by which America and Europe resemble each other: "the equality of conditions." Traits particular to America serve only to guarantee the tranquil and uninterrupted reign of this equality that, in the New World, reveals itself with all the force of "a generative fact,"[19] determining or at least modifying all aspects of political and social life.[20] In the New World, the equality of conditions is the "generative cause of laws and mores,"[21] manifesting itself without constraint or serious disruption from other influences. Contrary to the thinking of many of Tocqueville's contemporaries who belong to an aristocratic milieu, democracy is not simply disorder that leads to the dissolution of any healthy social life; it is, rather, the comprehensive principle of a new society. The equalization of conditions can be considered the leadwire of European history, because equality of conditions is the generative fact of the American republic, the daughter of Europe.

Chapter 1

THE DEFINITION
OF DEMOCRACY

> Among the new objects that drew my attention during my
> stay in the United States, none so keenly struck me as the
> equality of conditions. I readily discovered the prodigious
> influence that this premier fact exercised on the conduct
> of society. . . . Soon I recognized that this same fact ex-
> tends its influence well beyond political mores and laws.
> . . . It creates opinions, gives birth to sentiments, suggests
> customs, and modifies all that it does not produce. . . . I
> saw more and more in the equality of conditions the gen-
> erative fact from which each particular fact seemed to be
> derived. . . . When I turned my thought back to our hemi-
> sphere, it seemed to me that I could make out something
> analogous to the spectacle that the new world offered me.
> I see equality of conditions which, without having attained
> its extreme limits as in the United States, each day ap-
> proaches them more.[1]

Tocqueville distills his discovery of the essence of modern society, of democracy, in this way. The equality of conditions
is not a single characteristic among others, however important
they may be; it is the "generative fact" from which all the rest
is deduced. Modern societies have a "principle"[2] to which
everything that characterizes them must be referred. Certainly,
some of their traits have other origins,[3] but their specific dif-

1

ferences inhere in this principle and its effect. Equality of conditions is the common center of democratic societies, and it prevails in them all, more or less. This generative fact develops more or less freely and has consequences more or less complete. But it is to this fact that one must direct oneself to understand democracy.

It is obvious that modern societies exhibit widely different political regimes. Compare the French regime with the American regime, for example. The first is characterized by a centralized administration, precarious freedoms, and frequent and violent changes among those who hold supreme power. The second is characterized by administrative decentralization, recognized freedoms, and regular elections. The "generative fact" of equality defines a "social state," not a political regime. This does not mean that such a state has no political consequences— quite the contrary. But these political consequences manifest themselves in the form of an alternative.

> The political consequences emanating from a similar social state are easy to deduce. Equality will end up by penetrating the political world, as other realms. It is impossible to understand things otherwise. Now, I only know two ways to cause equality to reign in the political world. Rights must be given to each citizen or to no one. For peoples who have come to the same social state as the Anglo-Americans, it is therefore very difficult to see a middle course between the sovereignty of all and the absolute power of one.[4]

Two types of regimes, therefore, and only two can be established on this social base. In light of these alternatives themselves, Tocqueville summons men to their responsibility of choosing between the two great possibilities consequent upon the democratic social state.[5]

Therein lies a difficulty, insofar as Tocqueville does not stop insisting on the determinative force of this "generative fact," or on its "prodigious influence." It is, so to speak, the definition of the social state that it is the determinative cause, because Tocqueville renounces a search for what could determine the

2

definition in turn. "The social state is ordinarily the product of a fact, sometimes of laws, more often of the two causes combined. But once it exists, one can consider it the leading cause of the majority of the laws, customs, and ideas that regulate the conduct of nations. . . ."[6] How are we to reconcile this primary cause with the substantive freedom left to men to choose between the liberty of all and the despotism of one? What does it mean, to take responsibility for the political consequences of the social state?

"The first subjected to this terrible alternative, the Anglo-Americans, have been fairly fortunate in escaping absolute power. Circumstances, their origins, their intellectual lights, and above all, their mores, allowed them to found and maintain the sovereignty of the people."[7] Describing democracy in America means not only describing equality of conditions, it also means describing the sovereignty of the people, which is based on equality of conditions. From this point of view, what distinguishes the United States is that "in America, the principle of the sovereignty of the people is not hidden or sterile, as with certain other nations. It is recognized by mores, proclaimed by its laws. It expands freely and reaches its utmost development without obstacles."[8] This was the prevailing situation at the time of the founding: ". . . from the beginning, the principle of the sovereignty of the people had been the generative principle of the majority of English colonies of America."[9] In such a way, Tocqueville employs the very terms he used to describe the social state to characterize the importance of the sovereignty of the people in the United States. As with the social state, the sovereignty of the people is a "generative principle." The principle of the sovereignty of the people was previously characterized as one of two possible political consequences that could be derived from the democratic social state. Here, significantly, it seems that politics, under the rubric of sovereignty of the people, becomes a cause of itself.

Tocqueville shows us this principle emerging from local government to take hold of the "government of society" and become "the law of laws."[10] It is "in our time that the principle of

3

the sovereignty of the people has taken all the practical developments that imagination can conceive."[11] It seems that American democracy can be wholly understood by beginning from the principle of the sovereignty of the people. Beginning from the social state, Tocqueville places before us two alternatives, of which sovereignty of the people is one. Beginning directly from the sovereignty of the people, he presents the unequivocal "law of laws" of the American regime. The primordial political definition of democracy appears, according to the very terms of Tocquevillian analysis, more immediately and completely comprehensive than the definition of democracy by social state. If an elaboration of all consequences of the sovereignty of the people explains to such an extent democracy in America, what remains of the necessity to see the generative fact in the social state?

To make the scope of this question precise, it is appropriate to observe how Tocqueville describes the process by which the principle of the sovereignty of the people conquered the English colonies of America. We know that the principle was at first realized only at the local level. Its spread encountered two obstacles. One was foreign: the political subordination of the colonies to the mother country. The other was domestic: the aristocratic influences that were still active in the colonies. With the Revolution, the foreign obstacle was overcome, and the "dogma of the sovereignty of the people emerged from the locality to take hold of the government."[12] The law of succession obliterated the domestic obstacle. Of course, the law of succession belongs to the civil order and refers to the social state.[13] It follows that its role was only to remove the obstacle that blocked the spread of the principle of the sovereignty of the people to the whole of society. The principle of the sovereignty of the people is indeed a political principle, but it first prevailed in a politically subordinate element of the American society, and even there encountered social obstacles. It is this democracy, at the community level, that "lies at the root of the great social enigma"[14] in the United States. Thus, between the pole of the social state and the pole of the government is the local

4

community, which is the basic element of society, but this basic element is organized and governed *politically.*

Tocqueville appears to hesitate between two characterizations of democracy, one essentially social and one essentially political. In a sense, this hesitation is only a reflection of the intermediate status of the American local community. "The federal form of government in the United States appeared last. It was only a modification of this smaller republic, a condensation of political principles widespread throughout the entire society, preceding and existing independent from it."[15] What appears to define American democracy is neither the social state nor the governing political authority, but the political principle of the sovereignty of the people "widespread throughout the entire society." At the end of Chapter Four, *"Of the Principle of the Sovereignty of the People in America"* and the beginning of Chapter Five, *"The Necessity of Studying What Took Place in the Individual States Before Speaking About the Government of the Union,"* in the first part of the first volume, Tocqueville draws distinctions among three types of regimes: those where power is external to society (absolute monarchies and despotism, we may assume), those where it is both internal and external to society (aristocracies)[16] and, finally, the United States, where the society "acts by itself on itself," because "there is no power except what emanates from within."[17] He is painting the picture of a regime where the social bond is immediately political.

Tocqueville devotes the lengthy Chapter Five to an examination of the modes of action of these "political principles widespread throughout the entire society." From this examination, three essential characteristics can be deduced. The first is that this power is, in a certain sense, invisible. "In America, the laws are seen, their daily execution is perceived, everything is in movement around you, but the motor is discovered nowhere. The hand which directs the machine continually escapes detection."[18] However, at the same time, this invisible power is more present and active than elsewhere. "In the New England states, the legislative power extends to more objects than among us."[19] The result can be found in the following paradox.

5

"In the United States, government centralization is at its high point. It would be easy to prove that national power there is more concentrated than it has been in any of the ancient monarchies of Europe."[20] Thus, in the United States, there is power only within society but, at the same time, this invisible power that society exercises by itself on itself is more present, more active, and greater than any other power known in Europe.

Also in Chapter Five, Tocqueville describes social power under the kinds of power belonging to legislative bodies in the states. In Chapter Eight (the first part of the first volume), which no longer treats the government of the states but the *Federal Constitution*, he presents this social power under other modalities, in particular in the paragraphs devoted to establishing *"How the Position of President in the United States Differs from that of a Constitutional King in France."* After noting the principal differences, he writes the following:

> However, above the one as above the other, remains a directing power, that of public opinion. The power is less defined, less recognized, less formulated into laws, in France than in the United States. But it exists in fact. In America, it makes itself felt through elections and decrees; in France, by revolution. Despite the differences of their constitution, France and the United States have this point in common, that public opinion is in both, at end, the dominant power. Thus the generative principles of the laws are truly the same within these two peoples, although its development in one and the other place is more or less free, and the effects that issue from it are often different.[21]

Therefore, after the social state and the sovereignty of the people, we meet a third definition of the "generative principle" of democracy: the influence of public opinion, which is comparable to the influence of the social state insofar as one is, like the other, beyond the reach of the differences in political institutions. As with the social state, Tocqueville says that the Americans and the French experience different "effects" from public opinion. But at the same time, the power of public opinion is a form of the sovereignty of the people—unregulated, wild, but effective. "This principle, by its nature, is republican."[22] Public opinion, insofar as it is a generative principle of democracy, combines characteristics of the social state and the sovereignty of the people. Democracy can not be described except by combining, instead of separating, what is social and what is political. Tocqueville has recourse to vague expressions to designate this fact—social power, the action of society on itself. But these vague expressions nevertheless adequately describe what belongs to democracy.

Tocqueville is striving to elucidate the same thing in successively designating the social state, the sovereignty of the people and, finally, public opinion as the generative principle of the mores and laws of American democracy. It is necessary to try to discern the source that is common to these modalities, governed by the same principle.

The democratic social state is defined by equality of conditions: the absence of an aristocracy of birth and, more generally, the absence or at least the great weakening of "individual influence."[23] Tocqueville summarizes the dogma of the sovereignty of the people thus: "Each individual forms an equal portion of the sovereignty and equally participates in the government of the state. Each individual is therefore supposed to be as enlightened, as virtuous, and as strong as any other of his fellow men. He obeys society because union with his fellow men seems useful to him."[24] It is this doctrine that daily gives force to the public opinion that "reigns"[25] over American society. This is why one should not attach too much importance to the representative form by which the will of the people is expressed. The "representatives" of the American people have no latitude in which to move. "It is really the people who lead, and even though the form of government is representative, it is obvious that the opinions, prejudices, interests, and even the passions of the people can find no lasting obstacles that prevent them from making themselves felt in the daily direction of society."[26] The traditional distinction between direct democracy and representative democracy, between ancient democracy and mod-

7

ern democracy,[27] in fact shows itself utterly irrelevant to America. Thus, the democratic social state, like equality of conditions, prevents society from being subject to the directing influences of individuals or political groups. All American institutions are based on the idea of the sovereignty of the people. However, the force of public opinion changes this idea into everyday reality. To understand democracy in America means understanding in *"What Way One Can Really and Truly Say that in the United States It Is the People Who Govern."* (This is the title of the chapter that opens the second part of the first volume of *Democracy.*) The people only govern if, in every domain of life, each individual obeys only himself, either as a particular individual in what is strictly personal or as a member of the sovereignty, as coauthor of the general will, in what concerns the public good. This is what happens in America.

In the United States, the dogma of the sovereignty of the people is not an isolated doctrine which is unrelated to habits or the body of dominant ideas. On the contrary, one can envision it as the last link in the chain of opinions which envelop the whole of the Anglo-American world. Providence has given to each individual, whatever he is, the level of reason necessary for managing his own affairs with regard to what exclusively concerns him. In the United States, this is the great maxim on which rests political and civil society—the father demonstrates it to his children, the master to his servants, the local government to its administrators, the State to its counties, the Union to the States. Applied to the whole of the nation, it becomes the dogma of the sovereignty of the people. *Thus, in the United States, the generative principle of the republic is the same which directs the majority of human actions.*[28] (My emphasis.)

Thus one can say that the generative principle of democracy in America is, properly speaking, neither political nor social. It joins the political and the social only because, beyond one and the other, it determines "the majority of human actions." The sovereignty of the people is the *fundamental opinion* according to which Americans see the world and perceive their tasks, rights, and duties in this world. It is the matrix of opinion, the maxim of actions, the horizon for all undertakings. The Americans live in a democracy because they see the world and act in the world according to the principle of the sovereignty of the people. The uniqueness of their regime resides in the total hold that this principle has on their entire life.

The democracy that Tocqueville describes was foreseen by Montesquieu, but as democracy's extreme and dissolute form. In Chapter Three of Book VIII of *The Spirit of the Laws*, entitled *"Of the Spirit of Extreme Equality,"* he writes: "Such is the difference between an ordered democracy and one that is not, that, in the first one is equal only as a citizen and that, in the other, one is still equal as a magistrate, senator, judge, father, husband, master." The "spirit of extreme equality" that is, in the eyes of Montesquieu, a corruption of ancient democracy is, in Tocqueville's eyes, the very principle of American democracy. In America, the political law of democratic equality penetrates into social and family relations (masters and servants, fathers and children) that the traditional idea of democracy would judge as belonging to an equality proper to civic life alone. The characteristics that define citizen relations—liberty and equality—penetrate all aspects of human life in order to direct them. But at the same time, the relations that may properly be seen as civic are conceived as relations not of law but of nature because men are by nature equal and free. As a consequence, "man" and "citizen" become equivalent and interchangeable terms.

All human bonds are politicized at the same time that the political bond is naturalized. To say the same thing more precisely, the influence of one individual on another (in whatever kind of relationship) can be exercised legitimately only if it conforms to the principles that govern relations between equal citizens. In turn, the relations that prevail between equal citizens are only one specific kind of relationship that must by nature prevail between two men, whoever they are and in whatever kind of relation they find themselves. The generative principle of this society tends to guarantee against any action by any of its members being done out of obedience or even in deference to the will or influence of another, unless he is explicitly authorized by the general will to require the first to perform this act. In such a society, the acts of each have only two legitimate sources: personal will or the general will.

We now can appreciate why Tocqueville begins his presentation of American democracy by defining it by its social state, a definition that appeared less precise, less complete than defining it by the notion of sovereignty of the people. It is quite true that the definition by social state is less precise and complete. But it leads us more directly to what specifically distinguishes democratic society from all other societies. Other societies, or at least all European societies before democracy, including even the ancient cities of Greece and Rome,[29] were held together by the power of an inequality of conditions, by direct rule, and by the widespread influence that certain families exercised over the rest of society. The basic element of these societies was not the equality of one individual to another; it was the basic inequality of one family to another. They were formed by groupings of families united by obedience or, at least, deference to an aristocratic family placed higher in the social hierarchy. What held together societies that preceded democratic society was a hierarchy of patronage.

It follows that to define democratic society by equality of conditions is to uncover the root of what distinguishes it from other societies in European history. Democratic society is thus presented as a society founded on the absence of patronage, of family influences, however slight their strength or duration, a society that gives itself the task of living and prospering without reverting to this social link, which was universal before democracy and was defined by the dominance of powerful nobles or first citizens. To both realize and give expression to the fact of living together without obedience or deference to a small number who personify its identity, incorporate its excellence, and govern the destiny of the social body, is to introduce into human history a radical mutation of the social bond, in light of which the political regimes that tradition judged as distinctly different now appear different only in their nuances. Because Tocqueville has the most vital perception of this mutation, he can combine species from the same aristocratic genus—Athenian democracy and the European *ancien régime.* Modern democracy strikes out at and overturns that which changes in religion, political regime, or social organization had until then essentially left intact.

Putting the finishing touches to his description of the *"Social State of Anglo-Americans"* (Chapter Three of part one, volume I), Tocqueville writes the following: "Time, events, and laws have rendered the democratic element there, not only preponderant, but in a manner of speaking, the only one. No influences of family or social group let themselves be seen. Oftentimes, one can not even discover individual influences, so transient are they."[30] In this short chapter (less than nine pages), the word influence is employed six times. The progress of democracy is coincidental to the erosion of individual influences. A fully democratic social state is a social state in which there are no more individual influences. These formulations have to be taken literally, for in them are condensed the most novel and liveliest aspects of the Tocquevillian vision. In this context, at least, there is nothing to distinguish between aristocratic influences or patronage and individual influences of another kind, intellectual or moral, for example. Certainly, an intellectual or moral influence is not in itself an aristocratic influence. Tocqueville indicates that even in New England, individual influences can be seen that in no way belong to aristocracy. "The very seed of aristocracy was never sown in this part of the Union. One could only establish certain intellectual influences there. The people became accustomed to revere certain names, as the symbol of enlightenment and virtues. The voice of some citizens exerted on it a power that one could reasonably call aristocratic, if it could have been uninterruptedly transmitted from father to son."[31] But these intellectual influences, which could find space only in the democracy of New England because they fell short of aristocracy, were destined to perish with

11

the expansion of democracy because they rest on individual influences. Here, in effect, is what Tocqueville writes about the final end of American democracy: "It is in the West that one can observe democracy having come to its extreme limit. In these states, improvised by fortune in a certain sense, the inhabitants arrived yesterday on the soil they occupy. They hardly know each other and each one is ignorant of the history of his closest neighbor. In this part of the American continent, the population there escapes not only the influences of great names and great wealth, but also that natural aristocracy derived from enlightenment and virtue. The new states of the West already have inhabitants. But a society does not yet exist."[32] In such a way, Tocqueville anticipates the common-sense objections that a society that did not have individual influences would not be a society but a "dis-society." In a sense, this is the case with democracy. This limit of democracy is not the truth about democracy. Certainly, the states of the West, pioneer states, present some singular characteristics. It is only the more striking that Tocqueville sees in these the limits of democracy. It is the exaggerated image of democracy. The radical severing of the social links that democracy introduces opens us to the image of democracy as a "dis-society."

Chapter 2

DEMOCRACY
AND ARISTOCRACY

However legitimate the distinctions by which we tradition-
ally classify political regimes, the radical novelty of democracy forces the recognition of a more fundamental distinction, a polarity between two social states, one characterized by
equality of conditions, the other by inequality of conditions,
one democratic, the other aristocratic. The key to *Democracy
in America* can be found in the constant comparison, implicit
and explicit, between democratic society and aristocratic society, between a society where individual influences have never
existed and were never known, and one where they dominate.
The advantages and disadvantages of democracy must be
weighed against the advantages and disadvantages of aristocracy. Nowhere, however, does Tocqueville elaborate upon the
"generative principles" of aristocracy, as he does for democracy, and we know that the very idea of a social state as a generative fact came to him through observing American democracy. Certainly, Tocqueville deduces the host of consequences
he does—political, moral, and psychological—from the democratic social state. It even could be said that the second volume
of *Democracy in America* in its entirety is constituted by the
portrayal of two human types, aristocratic man and democratic man. But this symmetry is somewhat deceptive. The image
of the aristocrat is drawn only because the portrait of demo-

13

cratic man requires it. And while in the first chapter of this study, our attention has been engaged by the multitude of definitions of the fundamental ground of democracy, in the case of aristocracy, we are not exposed to such an embarrassment of riches. Our sole point of departure is contained in the formulation that links inequality of conditions and individual influences. Thus, we have to see how the light shed by Tocqueville on the nature of democracy delivers us from the shadows cast by aristocracy.

In the two volumes of *Democracy*, the word "aristocracy" makes an appearance in a title but once, even though the titles of many chapters and subsections are often quite long. This happens in the final subsection of Chapter Two, part two, of volume I, *"Parties in the United States."* In Chapter Two, he notes that "parties are an inherent evil in free governments." It is necessary to make a distinction, he continues, between the great parties "which are animated more by principles than their consequences" and that "generally have a more noble allure," and "small parties," which "agitate" and "corrupt" society. Tocqueville writes: "America has had great parties. Today, they no longer exist. It has been a gain in happiness but not in nobility. When the War of Independence reached its end, and the question was the establishment of a new government, the nation found itself divided between two opinions. These opinions were as old as the world, and one finds them under different forms and assuming different names in all free societies. One wants to restrain popular power, the other to extend it indefinitely."[1] These two parties were the *Federalists* and the *Republicans.*

The Federalists were vanquished necessarily because "they struggled against the irresistible inclinations of their century and their country,"[2] which went in the direction of concentrating social power. But thanks to their virtues and talents, they were able to imprint their wisdom upon the Constitution of the United States.

Thus, the aristocratic party was essentially vanquished. However, the epithet "aristocratic" had not become totally meaningless in the United States.

14

When one comes to study the secret instincts in America that govern factions, one readily discovers that the majority among them are to a greater or lesser degree linked to one or the other of the great parties that divided men ever since there were free societies. As one enters more deeply into the inner thoughts of these parties, it can be seen that one works to constrain the use of public power, the other to extend it. I am not saying that American parties always have as their ostensible object or even as a hidden object to cause aristocracy or democracy to prevail in their country. I am saying that aristocratic or democratic passions are readily found at the bottom of all parties and that although they may be hidden from view there, they make of them their vital center and soul.[3]

These lines confirm two very remarkable things. First, in a complete democracy, where the seeds of aristocracy have never been sown, the aristocracy/democracy distinction remains the key to political life. Despite the unopposed dominance of the democratic social state, aristocratic and democratic individuals are still identifiable. Next, Tocqueville equates the aristocratic party and the restriction of public power on the one hand and the democratic party and the expansion of social power on the other. It follows that even though the notion of aristocracy has lost all social significance, lost its proper and constitutive meaning, it conserves, it seems, a political significance of primary importance: opposition to the central power. By linking the two contrary attitudes regarding this power to the two great parties that "have divided men since there were free societies," Tocqueville seems to have cut loose the opposition aristocracy/ democracy from its original social understanding. The only notions taken into account here are liberty and public power. In fact, the attitude of democracy with respect toward public power stems from its social state, and accordingly, Tocqueville sees a demonstration of public power in the struggle between President Jackson and the Bank of the United States, which was raging at the time of his voyage.[4] He notes that the "enlightened classes" are in favor of the bank, while the people back the President. He makes the following comment: "Do you think that the people can discover the rational truth amidst all the twists and turns in such a difficult matter, and where even experienced men hesitate? In no way. But the Bank is a great institution with an independent existence. The people who bring down or raise up all powers can do nothing about it and that astonishes them."[5] In a democracy, any institution that is constructed to be independent of the immediate will of the majority has a powerful influence, which must be brought to obedience. Not only by its independence does such an institution effectively tend to disobey the general will, but even more, being in a position to exercise an influence on citizens themselves, it disturbs and falsifies the foundation of the general will. It encumbers the regular actions of society acting upon itself. Nothing in a democracy must escape the power of society over itself, of which the central power is the instrument and expression.

But because the aristocratic party was definitely vanquished, and this defeat was inevitable because the democratic social state necessarily forbade the survival or formation of aristocratic influences, the result of the combat between democracy and aristocracy's "vestiges" was preordained: *non parcere subjectis sed debellare istos.* In the absence of an aristocracy of birth, the rich alone can hope to exercise a distinctive influence, independent of—and eventually opposed to—democracy. They do not even attempt this. "The rich prefer . . . to abandon the competition rather than maintain an often unequal struggle against the poor and their fellow citizens. Not being able to assure a rank in public life analogous to that they occupy in private life, they abandon the first in order to devote themselves to the second. In the midst of the State, they form a society that has its tastes and joys apart."[6] One sees that the equality of conditions does not mean economic equality, since Tocqueville notes the presence of the rich in the United States. In addition, the fortunes of these rich are protected by the aura of respect that surrounds all property in this country.[7] But their wealth, as considerable as it is, remains something strictly private and does not guarantee a recognized public position from which they can exercise on their fellow citizens a power of opinion, a social influence substantially independent of the will of the majority, which is necessarily the will of the poor.[8] The members of the wealthier classes do not hold positions of authority in society *as members of these classes*. They, of course, can be elected by their fellow citizens to this or that public office, but then they are responsible to the people, and we have seen that these representatives do not have the power to exempt themselves for even the shortest time from the people's will. The democratic office holder can be a rich man, although even that will be somewhat rare;[9] while an office holder, he is the instrument of the majority.

The position of the aristocratic office holder is quite another thing. Public men in an aristocratic government have a class interest which, if it sometimes overlaps with that of the majority, remains distinct from it. Among them, this interest forms a common and durable bond. It encourages them to unite and combine their efforts toward a goal that is not always the good of the greatest number. It not only links the rulers with each other but it fully unites them with a considerable portion of the ruled, for many citizens, without having assumed any office of employment, are part of the aristocracy. The aristocratic officeholder, therefore, thus finds constant support in society, as he does in the government.[10]

We find again here the point that Tocqueville suggests at the end of Chapter Four of the first part of volume I when he spoke, without further elaboration, of countries "where power is divided, being at one and the same time, in society and outside of it."[11] In effect, such is the situation of a member of the aristocracy in a society founded on inequality of conditions. If he has a properly political position, his political power is the crowning symbol of the influence over the rest of society that he already holds as a member of the aristocracy. If he doesn't have a properly political position, he nonetheless exercises a power over his fellow citizens that would not be conceivable in a democracy, unless he had a properly political or at least public office. In other words, in an aristocratic society, the point where the so-

17

cial joins the political is entirely lodged in the aristocratic body. The consequences of this are that every member of this body occupies a position largely independent of the transient will of the holders of political power. Democratic society can tolerate no such a thing. It is a society that wants all to submit to—or at least be incapable of resisting—the immediate will of the majority of citizens. Nothing must come between the citizen as legislator and the citizen as subject. By virtue of his social standing, he finds himself independent of society, since he contributes to directing and influencing it, and of political power in the strict sense by reason of his social position. For his part, the man of democracy, independent of all individual influences, obeys the will of all, which he has contributed to forming equally with each of his fellow citizens. Both the aristocratic and democratic man can be said to be free, but in different ways.

Nowhere in *Democracy in America* does Tocqueville offer the faintest sketch of a comparison between these two sorts of liberty, although the distinction between democratic liberty and aristocratic liberty raises issues that lie at the heart of his vision. The only text that comes close to a systematic comparison is found in an article published in 1836 (thus a little after the appearance of the first volume of *Democracy*) in the *London and Westminster Review*, entitled *"The Social and Political State of France Before and After 1789."* There one reads the following:

> Liberty can appear . . . in the human spirit in two different forms. Liberty appears as the customary possession of a right or the enjoyment of a privilege. . . . This aristocratic notion of liberty (liberty as privilege) appears among those who have inherited an elevated sentiment of their individual value, an impassioned taste for independence. It gives to egoism an energy and a singular power. Experienced by individuals, it has often brought men to the most extraordinary acts. Adopted by an entire nation, it created the greatest people that ever existed. The Romans thought they alone in the human race were to enjoy independence. And it was much less from nature than from Rome

that they believed they held the right to be free. According to the modern idea, the democratic idea, and I dare say the correct idea of liberty, each man is presumed to have received from nature the lights necessary to govern himself, and possesses from birth an equal and inalienable right to live independent from his fellow men, in all that concerns himself only, and to decide his destiny as he understands it. . . . Each having an absolute right over himself, it follows that the sovereign will can emanate only from the union of the wills of everyone. From this moment on, it also follows that obedience has lost its moral character and there is no longer anything that separates the manly and proud virtues of the citizen from the lowly self-indulgence of the slave.[12]

It is fitting to quote this long statement as the most complete and explicit description by Tocqueville regarding the two liberties. Thus, democratic liberty corresponds to the correct idea of liberty. Consequently, it must be admitted that aristocratic liberty is founded on a false idea. This false idea, however, has good consequences, since it brings individuals to extraordinary acts and has created the greatest people that ever existed. On the other hand, the democratic idea, as correct as it is, tends to produce a precarious and menacing situation for individuals who find themselves thrown before a dangerous alternative between civic virtue and base servility. A correct idea of liberty tends to bring about bad consequences; a false idea of liberty tends to bring about good consequences. Such is the paradox that Tocqueville presents to us.

The aristocratic definition is immediately political, since it is as Roman citizens that Brutus or Cassius feel themselves to be free and wish themselves to be so. To be free and to belong to a particular political body called Rome is one and the same thing in their eyes. On the other hand, the democratic definition of liberty contains nothing specifically political. It only speaks of man and nature and, by nature, each man has an absolute right to govern himself. This definition invokes only the terms "man" and "nature," and addresses him as if he were in the state of nature. It speaks to him only of himself, but is meant to regulate his political relations with others. It addresses

the citizen as if he were without fellow citizens. Civic life presupposes permanent relations among individuals, although the
democratic idea of liberty begins by separating them. It follows
that ruling and being ruled, which are the very theme of political existence, can only be related to the supposedly solitary individual. To live democratically with one's fellow citizens is to
obey only oneself and therefore to command only oneself.
Never to obey the will of another that is not my own, nor to order another to do something that I am not disposed to do myself and that the other does not also will—such is the elevated
discipline that the democratic definition of liberty imposes.
Such are "the manly and proud virtues of the citizen." But it is
difficult to keep to these peaks. If because of softness, negli-
gence, or simple laziness, I agree to obey a will that does not
recognize mine, if I do what I do not will to do, I perform an act
that, in my own eyes, is neither legitimate nor moral. I lose my
self-esteem and I lend myself to the "lowly self-indulgence of
the slave." I am no better off in commanding what I am not disposed to obey myself than in commanding another to do something he does not assent to.

It is striking that, in sketching a definition of liberty as privilege as opposed to democratic liberty and also in the context of
an analysis of the French *ancien régime*, Tocqueville gives the
example of the Roman citizen. The civic tradition of the West
saw as incompatible the life of a citizen and the domination of
a landed aristocracy. In the course of centuries during modern
times, the traditional European order was often attacked in the
name of a civic ideal, the Roman or Greek ideal in particular.
However, what the aristocratic European order and the ancient
city had in common was the conviction that the simple fact of
being man is not a sufficient title to enjoy the right to liberty
and the other eminent advantages of political life. To put it
more crudely but more accurately, liberty can be conquered or
possessed by certain individuals only at the price of more or less
complete submission by others. The relations between the liberty of some and the non-liberty of others can of course vary
considerably according to the political body, as it is considered

both with regard to its internal organization and its relations with other political bodies. The liberty of ancient citizens was the counterpart of the almost total non-liberty of the slaves, in whom they found not only the conditions of their material existence but, even more, the reverse moral image by which liberty is apprehended and exalts itself as liberty. What gave ancient liberty its elevated taste was the hope of conquering and subjecting neighboring cities and the fear of becoming their slaves, in case of defeat. The political liberty of the European aristocrat is less complete than that of the ancient citizen because those in the *ancien régime* who are deprived of their liberty are freer than the slaves of antiquity and because foreign relations in the *ancien régime* are less dominated by the desire to subject others and the fear of being subjected by them than they were in the ancient city. The latter joins the extreme of liberty with the extreme of slavery.[13] The *ancien régime* combines a more moderate liberty with a more moderate slavery. This is why Tocqueville sees the model of liberty-as-privilege in the ancient city.

In the two cases, obedience to another is something according to nature. To obey is less honorable than to command, but it is not immoral. Otherwise, it would not be honorable to command. The world's subjection to the name of Rome can be a glorious thing only if the obedience of the people does not degrade them.

Tu regere imperio populos, Romane, memento
Hae tibi erunt artes pacisque imponere morem
Parcere subjectis et debellare superbos

In democratic society, on the other hand, obedience "loses its morality" insofar as the only legitimate obedience is obedience of a person to himself. Certainly, in a democracy, as in an aristocracy, men are held together by ruling and being ruled. But in an aristocracy, being ruled and ruling are apportioned to two different human groups in such a way that the one group and the other ordinarily develop complementary human functions,

21

the qualities and faults that belong to their habitual practices. Ruling brings out arrogance; obedience, servility. But it is in a man for whom ruling is second nature that one has the greatest chance to meet a rule where arrogance is absent and, above all, it is in a man for whom being ruled is second nature that one has the greatest chance of meeting an obedience without servility. In the first—democracy—being ruled and ruling are internal to each individual, who is at the same time both legislator and subject and who is supposed to adopt successively—even simultaneously—the posture of one who commands and one who obeys. Therein lies his high virtue that can accommodate two contrary habits.[14] The great majority of citizens has many more occasions to obey than to command. Therefore, they obey what one orders in the central power's name even when they do not recognize the morality of the obedience. They tend to servility before the central power, before the nominal will of the majority, because to obey is easier than to command or disobey and because obedience to the power of the majority is the only thing that allows them to entertain the illusion that they are obeying their own will. It thus follows that those who command and those who obey are hardly less distinct than they are in an aristocratic society. It is simply that the truth and morality of commanding, as with obeying, tends to be obscured, since those who command are supposed to obey and those who obey are supposed to command.

Such is the paradox of democratic liberty. It makes it more difficult for the civic virtues—mainly ruling and being ruled—to flourish at the same time that it makes demands upon them more imperious. The full impact of what the definition of democratic liberty entails makes its realization less probable. Worse—it naturally engenders behavior that is the enemy of liberty. Its definition, rightly understood and as it embodies justice, is found in the extension of the privilege of liberty to all citizens, which henceforth becomes a common right. It is liberty in the precise sense because it is equal liberty, and it is because it is equal that it engenders behaviors that are the enemy of liberty. In effect, the pith of the paradox lies in the following: In the formulation "liberty is equal for all," which essentially distills the definition of democratic liberty, the predicate is *stronger* than the noun. The extension of liberty to all members of the social body changes its meaning. The center of gravity of the social mechanism tips to the side of equality. To affirm the equal liberty of all citizens amounts to affirming equality first.

> An extreme point can be imagined where liberty and equality touch and fuse into each other. I am supposing that all the citizens participate in the government and that each has an equal right to participate in it. No one differs from his fellows: no one person can exercise tyrannical power. Men are perfectly free, because they are entirely equal. And they are all perfectly equal because they are all entirely free. It is toward this ideal that democratic peoples tend.[15]

This "ideal" is equivalent to the sovereignty of the people, which, as we have seen in Chapter One, is carried to its furthest extreme in America and is in turn equivalent to the democratic idea of liberty as articulated in Tocqueville's 1836 article, the democratic idea that puts liberty in peril. It follows that, in Tocqueville's eyes, the ideal of democratic liberty is simultaneously fulfilled and put in danger in democratic society. It is fulfilled with regard to its strongest inclination, equality, and it is put in danger with regard to its weakest, liberty.

How does the "ideal" actually operate in real society? It operates by separating individuals, since individual independence is only another name for the fusion of liberty and equality. The democratic ideal assures its hold on real society by isolating the members of the social body. At that point, each member is interested only in himself. Alone, the individual is weak. But he does not willingly contemplate acting with his fellow men because he is no longer interested in their fate. This is because the social state erodes individual influences. "Equality places men next to each other without any common bond to hold them together."[16] Thus, "this extreme point where liberty and equality touch and merge into each other," which is the "ideal" of democracy, is also the point where society dissociates, when each individual withdraws into himself. The democratic definition of liberty produces a democratic equality that separates men. Therein lies the threat.

> The vices that despotism engenders are precisely those that equality favors. These two things complement and encourage each other in a catastrophic way. Equality places men side by side with one another, without a common bond to hold them. Despotism erects obstacles between them and separates them. It predisposes them not to think about their fellow men and makes a kind of public virtue out of indifference. Despotism, which is dangerous at all times, is therefore particularly to be feared in democratic centuries.[17]

The "correct" definition of liberty that "merges" with equality liberates the effective power of equality while it hinders liberty. "They had wanted to be free in order to make themselves equal and insofar as equality takes deepest root with the aid of liberty, it makes liberty more difficult."[18]

Consequently, for democratic societies to know liberty, they must *add* liberty to that equality with which it appears to be united, not so much for the love of liberty itself but to give men the sentiment of society, the sentiment that they live together. "The free institutions that the inhabitants of the United States possess . . . in a thousand ways, incessantly remind each citizen that he lives in society."[19] Better yet, this liberty combats the bad effects of equality. "To combat the evils that equality can cause, there is only one effective remedy. That is political liberty."[20] The liberty and equality that merge in the democratic definition of liberty find themselves completely separated and even at least partially opposed.

Certainly this liberty, which is a remedy for the evils caused by equality, is established on democratic foundations, since its principal instrument is associations, by which equal individuals pool their money, time, and passions to realize whatever object of their desires. The goal of associations is to incessantly reknit the social fabric that equality of conditions continually tends to unravel. "The sentiments and ideas renew themselves, the heart strengthens and the human spirit develops only through the reciprocal action of men on each other. . . . This action is almost nonexistent in democratic countries. It is therefore necessary to create it artificially. And this is what associations alone can do."[21] A distinction is drawn between the role played by formal political associations and civil associations. "In the civil sphere, each individual can, if absolutely necessary, imagine his self-sufficiency. In the political sphere, this is never so. Therefore, political associations can be considered as great schools, free of charge, where all citizens come to learn the general theory of associations."[22] But if the political associations are the school of the associative spirit, the civil associations are more fundamental. "If men who live in democratic countries have neither the right or the taste to come together for political goals, their independence will run great risks, but they will be able to preserve their wealth and knowledge for a long time. While if they do not acquire the custom of association in day to day life, civilization itself will be imperiled."[23]

In such a way, one sees the hold of the ideal of democratic freedom on society unleash two developments. The first—derived from the principle that every man is fully sovereign only in what concerns himself while, in things that concern the whole social body, he obeys the will of the majority—gives rise to the brutal eradication or the slow erosion of the individual influences by which men are held together in aristocratic societies. While in the civil sphere this development liberates each individual from the influences of a more powerful neighbor, it assures the omnipotence of a majority will that does not allow any social power—of whatever importance—to withhold itself from what that will commands. The other development—less spontaneous, "artificial"—reknits through associations the social fabric, which is unraveled in the first instance, and strives to force the will of the majority to respect what these associations hold as important. The first process belongs to the "natural consequences of the democratic social state."[24] The second belongs to the political art of democracy, a political art particularly perfected in America.

Democracy, from the point of view of political art, thus has the task of fabricating what was *given* in aristocratic societies. "In aristocratic societies, men did not need to come together to act because they were already strongly held together. Each citizen, rich and powerful, formed there a head of a permanent and involuntary association composed of all those that it held in dependence and which it made contribute to the execution of its designs."[25] The union of men is one with the respective positions of individuals, with the inequality of conditions and the hierarchy of influences that such inequality entails. In a democracy, the union of its members becomes the very theme of the activity of individuals. To live in a democracy is not the condition of the life of individuals; rather, it becomes the goal in all aspects of existence.

To grasp well this dual character of democracy undoubtedly takes us furthest in understanding what is unique to the thought of Tocqueville: on the one hand—the irresistible necessity, "the natural consequences of the social state," the "instincts"[26] of democracy; on the other—the political art,[27] free association, the freedom of the press, all those institutions that characterized American democracy. These institutions, which seem to us to contain the very meaning of democracy, to illustrate its definition in a certain sense, were in Tocqueville's eyes, above all, artifices by which democracy arrives at gaining control *over itself*. "The Americans have shown that it is not necessary to despair about regulating democracy with the aid of laws and customs."[28]

Democracy undoes the social bond and reties it in another way. All the power of one man over another, founded on force, inherited prestige, and the prestige of personal qualities is irresistibly eroded. Two individuals are separated and placed side by side "without a common bond to hold them." That is the nature of democracy.

Democracy tends to place men in a kind of state of nature,

and it demands that they reconstitute society from this base. The real process of democracy as Tocqueville described it is almost the exact replica of the process of thought common to the principal theoreticians of the social contract: to criticize extant aristocratic institutions in the name of the elementary rights of the individual such as are deduced from—and prevail in—the state of nature; to elaborate on the idea of a pure state of nature where all relations among men would illustrate these rights; to show how men may leave the state of nature and create a society that does not violate these principles as does aristocratic society.

There are nevertheless two differences of unequal importance between the real process and the process of thought. The first is that the state of nature of democracy is a civilized state of nature, whereas the creation of society and civilization is one thing for contract theorists. We have seen that in the absence of civil association, civilization itself would be threatened. We have seen also that the democratic process contains within it the threat of a state of nature increasingly less civilized. The second difference is more important. Contract theorists make society's break with the state of nature *definitive*. The return to that state is envisioned as the dissolution of society—by definition exceptional and disastrous. Real democracy never ceases establishing the state of nature in order to continually abandon it. To establish a state in which truly independent men would be in a position to associate while at the same time preserving their liberties is its task—always unfinished. Incessantly, human relations, which in a previous phase of the democratic process appeared given and obvious, now reveal themselves as founded on a principle other than the free association of equal individuals. It is thus necessary to dissolve these relations in order to reconstitute them on a new basis. So it goes indefinitely. Moreover, free associations themselves, with time, tend to be unfaithful to their democratic foundation. It will thus be necessary to dissolve them also, then reconstitute them. Democratic society does not wish to "return to the state of nature." It wants to found itself on that state once that state is finally attained, because it wants to found itself beginning with free and equal individuals. The quest of that state is its primary task, its most imperative step, the basis of its legitimacy. The task of creating associations is by definition subordinated to that of creating—or refounding—effectively free individuals who alone can associate democratically. To establish the conditions of the creation of the only legitimate society is the social work of democracy.

The distinction between democracy as social state and democracy as political institution is not a matter of applying to democracy a general "sociological" distinction. The greater weight given to the social state is no longer a function of a causal superiority generally attributed to social authority over political authority. Nor, in the end, can the social and the political be considered as two "aspects" of democracy arbitrarily separated out of the solid mass of fact, or considered as two "conceptual levels," deliberately elaborated to make exposition easy for the observer of democracy. It is the very *stuff* of democracy that lends itself to this *real* duality.

Certain observers of democracy (and not the least influential) have presented democratic institutions—freedom of the press, of association, trial by jury—as formal in opposition to the real inequalities of this society. It is at the very heart of these inequalities that Tocqueville sees the great work of democracy in operation. If it is truly necessary to oppose real democracy and formal democracy, it is then fitting to say that formal democracy is the remedy for the evils produced by real democracy. Certainly, there are always rich and poor, masters and servants, but under the apparent continuity of the old hierarchies, having just been refurbished, all the traditional reference points of social life have been radically modified. What these eloquent censors of formal democracy have not been able to see is the force of democratic equality to which their indignation and doctrines in the end bear witness.

Chapter 3

THE FORCE
OF DEMOCRATIC EQUALITY

The most complete, explicit, and paradoxical text in which Tocqueville demonstrates the irresistible force of democratic equality and describes its mode of action is the chapter *"How Democracy Modifies the Relationship of Servant and Master."* If there is a relationship unequal by definition, it is certainly that of master to servant. Outside of slavery, properly understood, one can not imagine a more complete domination of one individual over another. Yet, this relationship, despite appearances, is not proof against democratic equality. "One has not yet seen societies where the conditions are so equal that rich and poor are not met and, consequently, masters and servants. Democracy does not prevent the existence of these two classes of men, but it changes their spirit and modifies their real relations."[1] To appreciate the modification of these relations, Tocqueville draws a detailed comparison between aristocratic and democratic household servants.

The ruling principle of aristocratic household service is the same as that of aristocratic society as a whole. "In the society of servants as in that of masters, men exert great influence on one another."[2] Each finds himself securely bound to his place. In the same manner as master keeps servants in their place, within the group of servants the ranks are fixed, and the rules of their petty public life established. Being born to such a sta-

29

tion and likely destined to die there, each plays his role with all
the pride it can bear. A double movement within the group of
servants is the consequence. On the one hand, there is an extension of the hierarchy of domination, no less rigorous among
the servants than between masters and of master to servant. On
the other hand, there is a diffusion of certain aristocratic virtues
from master to the group of servants, modified of course by the
diffusion. "These men, whose destiny is only to obey, undoubtedly do not understand glory, virtue, honesty, honor, in
the same way as the masters. But they develop a servant's glory,
virtues, and honesty, and they exhibit, if I may speak in such a
way, a sort of servile honor."[3] From this it follows that both the
society of masters and that of servants are animated, albeit according to different modalities, by the same aristocratic spirit,
with the exception, certainly, of those found in the lowest ranks
of the domestic class. "It is understood that the men who occupy the lowest end in a hierarchy of valets are exceedingly low.
The French invented a word expressly for the last of the line of
servants in an aristocracy. They called them lackeys."[4] Moreover, in conformity with the aristocratic principle, the social
positions are familial, not individual. "For several generations,
the same family of valets is established alongside the same families of master . . . which prodigiously modifies the mutual relationships between these two orders of people."[5] The master
comes to think of his servant as "an inferior or secondary part
of himself,"[6] while the servant ends up identifying himself with
the person of the master to such an extent that he comes to "lose
interest in his own self."[7] Thus, extreme social distance engenders a sort of assimilation and familiarity.

Democratic societies introduce social mobility. "There is still
a class of valets and a class of masters, but it is not always the
same individuals, nor especially the same families, which compose them. And there is nothing permanent in the status of
commanding or obeying."[8]

It follows that the group of servants is no longer modeled after that kind of aristocratic education adapted to its purpose
that prevailed in aristocratic societies. The servant no longer

has the vices or virtues of his predecessors. "I have never seen in the United States anything that could remind me of a service elite, but neither did I find there the idea of a kind of lackey."[9] From the moment the idea of equality is inscribed in laws and affirmed by public opinion, master and servant both regard their positions with different eyes. If one serves the other, it is by virtue of the only thing that could legitimate democratic obedience—the contract. The contract might well be judged a legal fiction, but it is through this fiction that the servant and finally the master also consider their relationship. The spirit of their relationship is thus changed. "It is in vain that wealth and poverty, positions of command and obedience, haphazardly set great distances between two men. Public opinion, which is founded on the commonplace order of things, brings them together on a common level and creates between them a sort of imaginary equality, in spite of the real inequality of their conditions."[10]

Because equality forms the horizon of the social conscience, extremely elevated or lowly positions appear "haphazard." Nothing in the social conscience supports keeping these extreme positions in their place. When Tocqueville opposes "imaginary equality" to "real equality," he is not suggesting that this equality is fictional or illusionary—quite the contrary. This "imaginary" phenomenon is that of "public opinion," and we know that in his eyes public opinion is the "generative principle" of democratic societies. Moreover, if Tocqueville does not go so far as to say that this "imaginary" equality will end by bringing about real equality, his whole analysis suggests that he nevertheless believes it. So much does the consciousness of men determine their existence that one century was enough for the abolition of domestic service in democratic societies.

While the conditions of master and servant come together, their personal attachments slacken. We have seen how aristocratic domestic service attaches the servant to the master, and in a certain sense, the master to the servant, and produces assimilation and familiarity. Nothing of the kind exists in democratic domestic service. Each tends to think of his position as

31

"haphazard" and therefore can not establish durable bonds with the other that a change of position—as improbable as it may be—would render untenable. The relationship between master and servant is no longer fixed, immutable, having a self-evident character that alone allows for sentiments to crystallize. "They forever remain strangers to one another."[11] It is the other who is familiar and the like who is foreign.

The principal effect of democracy is to render master and servant strangers to one another, altering their position so that they are no longer one well above the other, but side by side. Thus, the most inherently unequal relationship is thoroughly transformed by democracy. We see precisely here that to oppose real democracy to formal democracy goes right by the essential truth about democracy. In democracy, men are not equal in fact, nor are they equal "only" in rights. Between the right and the fact is found an intangible thing, "imaginary" but irresistible, which Tocqueville calls "public opinion." Public opinion places men who are apparently most unequal in an element of equality and similitude, just as it renders obsolete the distinction between direct democracy and representative democracy. Equality is the *sensorium commune* of democratic social life.

If on one hand, democratic equality irresistibly erodes traditional equalities and infiltrates the strictest relationships of domination such as the relation between master and servant on the other hand, it is necessary to realize that in democratic societies, new inequalities develop to such a degree that Tocqueville does not hesitate to envision *"How Aristocracy Could Emerge From Industry"* (D.A. II, Part 2, Ch. 20). He observes that the advance of the division of labor—which is indispensable to the development of industry—on the one hand makes the worker "weaker, more limited, and more dependent,"[12] while on the other leads the owner, because of the scope of his enterprise, to constantly enlarge his capacities. "Thus it is that at the same time that industrialized societies constantly degrade the working class, they elevate the industrial owning class."[13] Democratic mobility itself, which destabilizes the position of servant as it does master, does not affect the conditions of the worker. "It is in vain that laws and mores have been so assiduous in breaking all the barriers that hem in this man and to open to him on all sides a thousand different roads to fortune. An industrial principle more powerful than mores and laws attaches him to a job, and often to a place that he can not leave. In the midst of universal movement, it has made him immobile."[14] In such a way, at the very heart of industrial society, a new aristocracy suddenly seems to appear. "As the mass of the nation turns to democracy, the particular class involved in industrial production becomes more aristocratic. Men appear more and more alike in the one and more and more different in the other and inequality increases in the small society to the same degree that it decreases in society at large."[15]

If inequality increases in the industrial professions, if in some way a new aristocracy is created, "this aristocracy does not resemble the ones that preceded it."[16] While the traditional aristocratic principle informed the whole society, here it prevails only locally, in a limited segment of the social body, in such a way that this new inequality is "an exception, a monster, in the whole of the social state."[17] Not only is this aristocracy limited in scope, it is also different in character, in its principle. Certainly, the proletariat is almost as vigorously bound to its position as the oppressed of yore. But the new rich are not comparable to the former aristocrats. "Truly, although there were rich people, the class of the rich did not exist, for these rich people had neither a shared spirit or objects in common, nor tradition or hopes in common. There were therefore members but no social body."[18] Tocqueville writes that the class of rich does not exist because the rich in democratic societies do not constitute an aristocratic *corps* or body. But the paradox is this, by the same token, the worker depends on the class of the rich and not on an individual rich person. "The worker depends in general on the owning classes but not on a particular individual."[19] This is because the rich do not constitute the leading class in the full sense of the term, while the workers belong only to their class. Thus, the characteristics of the new inequality are born

33

of traits distinctive to democratic egalitarian societies. The rich no longer exert any influence over those they employ. "The aristocracy founded on commerce almost never establishes itself in the center of the industrial population that it directs. Its goal is not to govern them but to make use of them."[20] Because the rich do not govern the poor who depend on them, because no bond of familiarity attaches them to the poor, they are totally insensitive to their miseries. But at the same time, they have no hold over them and would undoubtedly lack the force that could keep them subjected for long. "The manufacturing aristocracy that we see rise up before our eyes is one of the hardest that has ever appeared on earth, but it is at the same time one of the most restrained and least dangerous."[21] This new aristocracy, therefore, is simultaneously particularly hard and particularly weak. These two contradictory traits are born of the same generative fact: the rich do not exert any individual influence over those they employ.

Thus, if the new inequality is a monster in the social state, its monstrous characteristics are born of this same social state. It is in the vacuum left by the collapse of traditional social dependence that the new inequality reveals itself. The rich and the poor come into contact as class against class because the rich have ceased to constitute a ruling class. The new inequality is the fruit of the new equality. It follows that the manifest destiny of the "small society" in industrial times is to obey the logic of the egalitarian democracy of society at large. The social metabolism by which democracy recreates in another fashion what it has undone will shortly intervene to transform the conditions of the working class. The mode of life of men who represent the weakest and most vulnerable in democratic society will be regulated by the legislator;[22] however, they themselves will find the means to associate in order to reconstitute among themselves the social link and to make their new insensitive masters feel their force. The rich, who no longer govern the weak, will no longer have sufficient influence over them to prevent this process. The new domination of the manufacturing aristocracy, if it is the negation of the equality of conditions, is also its fruit. It will be eroded by a double process—the intervention of the central state and the formation of associations—by which democratic societies are held together and through which they constantly remake the social fabric that equality of conditions undoes.

Certainly Tocqueville, if he foresees and even recommends the intervention of the legislator, hardly speaks of worker associations. What he writes of the nascent workers' movement[23] expresses a profound hostility and gives witness, perhaps, to the lack of sensitivity of an aristocrat of the old school almost equal to that of the new rich. But the development of workers' associations strictly conforms to the logic of democratic society as he has revealed it. The small space he allots to the new industrial inequality in his picture of democratic society suggests that, from his perspective, it will not be able to resist for long the force of the democratic equality of which it is the paradoxical and provisional product.

It follows in democracies that the principal dividing line between subject and ruler is not a product of the effects of the old surviving inequalities—radically subverted, like that of master and servant—nor even the new—contrary to social logic—and therefore only provisional, like that of capitalist and proletarian. What guides the destiny of societies is the dual process by which the principle of democracy undoes and remakes the social bond. The more society is broken down into its elements by the equality of conditions, the more it must, if it is to hold together, have recourse to a power that is external to it. But at the same time, in order for this power to have a hold on this society, because it is external, and the more it is external, this power must be the power of society acting on itself. The more democracy undoes the social bond, the more society reconstitutes itself outside of and beyond individuals thereby isolated. What Tocqueville designates by expressions like "social power," "the action of society on itself," is the process by which society dissociates the individuals who compose it in order to come to rule them from the outside—given that society is nothing without these individuals. One could say—and Tocqueville does—that democratic society is ruled by associations, by the central power, by public opinion, by the sovereignty of the people. All these formulations are true. But all these are but instruments, sometimes complicit, sometimes contradictory, to assure the hold of society over itself—the hold of the social power.

Chapter 4

THE SOCIAL POWER

We have seen that Tocqueville judges this social power, intrinsic to American democracy, as greater than all other power known in Europe. By what instrument, by what scale, can we measure the quantity of power? Are we not involved here with an arbitrary judgment, which expresses more the reserve of an aristocrat than the truth about democracy? Tocqueville answers: "When one examines the character of thought in the United States, it is then that one clearly sees to what point the power of the majority surpasses all other powers that we know in Europe."[1] It is by viewing its effects on the intellectual life that one discovers most clearly the scope of democratic social power, since by nature thought is the most elusive thing in the world, the most resistant to domestication. The experience of Europe seems to prove the impossibility of this domestication. "There is not a country in Europe so subject to a single power that someone who wishes to speak the truth does not find there a support capable of protecting him against the consequences of his independence. If he has the misfortune of living under an absolute government, he often finds the people on his side. If he lives in a free country, he can in case of need find protection under royal authority. The aristocratic element of society supports it in democratic countries and the democratic in others."[2] In all these regimes, as uncongenial as they otherwise may be to freedom of thought, social power is divided. The contrary is observed in the United States. "In the heart of a democ-

37

racy organized as in the United States, a single power is met, a single element of strength and a single way to succeed, and nothing exists outside it."[3] In effect, the grand lives of individuals, independent of political power, which characterize aristocracies, have been abolished here; rather, they have never existed. Centralized powers, like local powers, are the docile instruments of the will of the majority. There is no refuge for the rebel spirit in this society where all is one and wishes itself so.

To this we might object, as Tocqueville acknowledges, that individual liberties are better assured in the United States than in any other regime. That is true. In restraining thought, the American democracy neither employs physical constraint nor encumbers any liberty.

> The prince made violence palpable, so to speak. The democratic republics of our day have spiritualized it all as a matter of human will, which they wish to constrain. Under the absolute government of a single person, despotism, to reach the soul, strikes out at the body. And the soul, escaping these blows, raises itself gloriously above them. But in democratic republics, tyranny does not proceed in such a way. It leaves the body alone and goes straight to the soul.[4]

These striking and suggestive phrases grope to express an invisible constraint that exerts itself directly on the spirit, where thought is given birth and conceived before it is born. The phenomenon that Tocqueville is looking to describe is not a democratic variant of eternal conformity. To understand it, it is necessary to read together the paragraph under the title of *"Of the Power That the Majority in America Exercises on Thought"* (Chapter Seven, second paragraph, vol. I) and the two chapters that open volume II, successively entitled *"Of the Philosophic Method of the Americans"* and *"Of the Principal Source of Belief Among Democratic Peoples."*

Because man thinks, he can not live without having opinions about the world that surrounds him and about himself. The majority of these opinions are received by each person without question. This is why Tocqueville calls them "dogmatic beliefs."[5] This situation is "not only necessary but desirable."[6] In effect, "a man who undertakes to examine everything by himself could accord only a little time and attention to each thing. This work would throw his mind into a constant turmoil which would prevent him from deeply penetrating into any truth and establishing himself solidly in any certitude."[7] Consequently, "it is always necessary, whatever happens, that authority is met somewhere in the intellectual and moral world."[8] And the question in democratic societies, as in others, is not to know if there will be intellectual authority, but where it will be lodged.

Let us now recall the definition of the democratic social state. Equality of conditions means the end of individual influences. In such a society, a man can not exert great influence over another.

> With regard to the influence the intelligence of a man can have over another, it is necessarily very restrained in a country where the citizens, having become almost alike, all see each other extremely close up, and, not perceiving in any of them the signs of grandeur and incontestable superiority, are incessantly brought back to their own reason as towards the most visible and closest source of the truth. It is thus not only the confidence in such a man which is destroyed but the taste to even trust on face value any man whatsoever. Each person narrowly withdraws unto himself and has the pretension to judge the world from such a perspective.[9]

It can be seen that, as the initial analysis of the social state suggested,[10] the end of aristocratic influences endangers the intellectual and moral influences of those that Tocqueville already suggestively called "the natural aristocracy." It is this idea, the very matrix of the influence that one man has over another—whether it be that of "reason or virtue"—that is here destroyed.[11]

Surely, equality of conditions cannot abolish inequality of nature and intellectual inequality in particular. "Intellectual inequality comes directly from God and man cannot prevent it from continually manifesting itself."[12] Three times in the course of the book, Tocqueville directly links intellectual inequality to the imperious decree of the Creator.[13] But the man who is superior in intellect or virtues has a lot of trouble in such a social atmosphere: he finds it difficult to make contact with his fellow citizens, to act on them, to solicit their love for the truth or the good.

Given that "each withdraws unto himself and has the pretension to judge the world from such a perspective"—does such a prideful attitude promise independence of spirit? Not at all; rather, it promises vanity. In effect, I am as good as another. And especially, it necessarily follows that anyone who is separate from the influence of another is closed to what comes from outside. Separated from the influences of another, he has no access to the things themselves, because to know things, a person has to go outside himself, and this is something only one's better can teach. The changes in the relations of men change the relations of men to things.

But how could democratic man, weak and isolated, really have faith in himself? He is as good as another, but this other is as good as he is. He can believe only in himself, but he has no faith in himself. It follows that he does not trust himself or another, but a third that they form together, at one with all others. They trust in the masses. "As citizens become more equal, the disposition to believe in the mass of individuals increases. . . . In times of equality, men have no faith in one another because of their similarity. But this same similarity gives them an almost unlimited confidence in the judgment of the public. This is because it does not seem likely that truth would not be found on the side of the greatest number, since everyone has a similar perspective on it."[14]

It follows that what democratic man believes in is not himself, nor another man, nor a class, nor a church. It is this something that is not thought by anyone personally and that one therefore may believe thought by all. That is called "opinion." In all societies, there are common opinions. But it is only in democratic society that this common opinion prevails unopposed, for the other possible sources of opinion have lost their credibility. This is why "not only is common opinion the sole guide that remains for individual reason with these democratic peoples, but it has with these peoples a power which is infinitely greater than with any other people."[15]

It is this common opinion that exerts a constant and almost irresistible pressure on the spirit and soul of each individual. What is more, it is the opinion of the "sovereign," which in this case is everywhere, and "everywhere accessible." "The democratic republics bring the spirit of courts to the level of the greatest number and cause it to penetrate in all classes at the same time."[16] Each individual is both a member of the court and is courted in turn and takes on the vices belonging to both circumstances in the midst of this common mass that "lives in perpetual adoration of itself."[17]

On the basis of this analysis, Tocqueville thinks himself on solid ground when he makes the following judgment. "I do not know a country where there reigns in general less independence of spirit and true free discussion than in America."[18] It is this absence of intellectual freedom that illustrates the incomparable scope of the social power that is exercised in democracies. One sees that this social power is held by all and by no one, and that it is exercised over all. Every individual obeys it, but in obeying, he obeys only himself—himself as a member of this mass, this conglomerate of "similar individuals," the source of all authority. Certainly, Tocqueville most often expressly identifies this social power in political terms, as the "omnipotence of the majority" or its "tyranny." But by dint of the very process we have just analyzed, each individual wishes himself a member of the majority and feels himself constrained or obligated to obey it. Certainly, on each political question subject to a legislative decision, majority and minority viewpoints emerge. But the pressure of social power renders this opposition more and more limited, so that the opinions of Americans "differ only in nuances."[19] The more that democratic social power makes its pressure felt, the more majority dogma prevails, the more the difference blurs between the principles and goals of the majority and the minority. The omnipotence of the majority in America is only the political and juridical expression of the omnipotence of society, characteristic of democratic nations.

One sees how the absence of freedom of thought in the United States differs in nature but not degree from ordinary conformity. It is not simply a question of bending to an opinion because it is commonly held, but that a legitimate opinion exists only because it is commonly held. The manner by which Tocqueville puts forth the example of religion is significant. In the Christian monarchies of Europe, the authority of religion resides in its revealed character, whatever the supplementary support brought to it by simple social conformity or prudence. In the chapter that opens volume II of *Democracy*, Tocqueville writes: "Christianity has retained a great Empire over the spirit of Americans, and what I wish above all to point out is that it reigns not only as a philosophy that one adopts after examination but as a religion that one believes without discussion."[20] Several pages further on, we read: "If one looks at it closely, one could see that religion itself there [in the United States] reigns much less as revealed doctrine than as common opinion."[21] If religion in the United States is not accepted upon examination but held as a dogma, the legitimating source of this doctrine is not revelation but common opinion. It follows that the hold exercised over individuals is even greater. Tocqueville went so far as to write: "The Inquisition could not prevent books contrary to the religion of the greatest number from circulating. In the United States, the empire of the majority does better. It has dared to go so far as to remove the thought of publishing them."[22]

The power of the democratic social state does not limit itself to concentrating in common opinion the whole intellectual authority. Society is not simply a reality and force external to thought. Rather, it tends to become the constitutive theme, the texture of thought itself. The democratic social state transforms the very substance of ideas that occupy the spirit of men. It produces new and particular ideas and modifies the rule and the matter of men's intellectual activity.

Each individual sees, wants to see, and can only see similar individuals around him. This is why "all the truths which apply to himself appear to him to apply equally or in the same manner to each of his fellow citizens and his counterparts."[23] To think about human things, he spontaneously reverts to general ideas and the more these ideas are general, the more they answer his expectations. In such a way, there nourishes and grows the "need to discover in all things common rules, to classify a great number of objects in the same category, and to explain a whole host of facts by a single cause," a need that becomes "an ardent and blind passion of the human spirit."[24] From this arises "a constant use of generic terms and abstract words."[25] This tendency is not without certain inconveniences. "The abstract words which fill democratic languages and which one makes use of at every turn without linking them to any particular fact, inflate and cover over thought. It renders expression more rapid and the idea less clear."[26]

But there are political dangers graver than imprecision and vagueness of thought. In egalitarian centuries, as all citizens are independent of one another, and each is weak, "one cannot make out the will which permanently moves the crowd. In these times, humanity seems always to move along under its own auspices."[27] It is thus that the historians in democratic centuries are inclined to subject human history to a system of general causes. Now "a cause which is vast enough to apply to millions of men and strong enough to bind them all at the same time and incline them all in the same direction readily seems irresistible."[28] There lies the great danger, for if the doctrine of historic inevitability takes hold of the mind of men, "one can see that it would soon paralyze the movement of new societies and reduce Christians to Turks."[29]

Thus, democratic social power tends to reduce the effective intellectual freedom of individuals and at the same time to convince them that individual liberty has little hold and significance, to convince them that all processes—and human history in particular—obey a rigorous necessity where man is absent. It follows that this power that reduces freedom is indistinguishable from the ideas that give rise to and maintain the democratic social state in the minds of men. And if it is greater than all other known powers, this is the case essentially because it operates in a radically different fashion, entirely lodged in the element of thought and perception. It does not exert influence in spite of individuals; it is only the realization—the concrete development—of the perception that democratic individuals have of their social world. Given that all legitimacy is supposed to reside in number, to think like others is not only easy, nor even an external obligation, it is the very horizon of the individual's mind-set. The only protests of any importance against conformity and the democratic consensus are made in the name of the social ideal that advocates a more complete uniformity, a more advanced resemblance.

Certainly, the legitimacy of number can be linked to any thought at all from the moment this thought becomes that of the majority, as the situation of Christianity in the United States testifies. Christianity was born well before the appearance of democracy, took root in the West during the aristocratic epoch, and has been chosen by the American masses as a religion under which they wished to live, and within the circle of its power they wanted others to live. But the crucial point is that this formal legitimacy tends to become materially operative and to transform the contents of thought that it legitimates. Thus it gives rise to its own perception of the social world. The ultimate presupposition of the majoritarian idea is that what is the most just lies with the idea of the strongest. This *very thing* by which democratic men resemble each other more and more, this very thing through which they think and perceive themselves, this very thing that is dearer and more intimate than themselves, is nothing human. They can only think it and represent it to themselves in positing it as outside themselves, an irresistible force that pushes and calls to them, a power so much more penetrating than it would be were it their own: the necessity of history, mass power without limit, the irresistible grip of society.

The hold of the idea of the equal individual on the perceptions of democratic man is such that even the idea of the tyranny of the majority seems to be too weak a notion. It is, so to speak, a transformation of the condition of man as Tocqueville describes it to us, and it affects his sentiments and passions as much as his ideas and perceptions.

Chapter 5

THE MILDNESS
OF DEMOCRACY

For several centuries, we have seen conditions becoming
more equal and we discover at the same time that mores
have softened. Are these two things only coincidences, or
does there exist some secret link, so that one cannot advance without operating on the other? There are several
causes which can contribute to making the mores of a people less rude. But among all the causes, the most powerful
appears to me to be equality of conditions. The equality of
conditions and the softening of mores are therefore not
only in my eyes contemporary events, they are even more
correlative facts. . . .

Tocqueville makes this statement in the chapter that opens
the third part of Volume II of *Democracy*, dealing with
"The Influence of Democracy on Mores in the Precise Sense."
The softening of mores does not therefore appear to him as a
contingent fact, somehow linked to a general cause external to
democracy, such as the progress of thought. He links the softening directly to the profound logic of the democratic social
state. He gives as a counterpart the example of the insensitivity and "cruel jesting" of a Mme. de Sévigné. He asserts that
this cruelty belonged neither to a defect of her person nor a lack
of enlightenment in the century when she lived, but to the aristocratic social state.

In effect, in an aristocratic society, diverse social groups each have their own mores and habits, an existence "apart." "Individuals become so progressively dissimilar, that one could say that there are as many distinct kinds of human beings as there are classes."[1] In such a society, "the general idea of a *fellow man* grows obscure."[2] Now, "there are real sympathies only between similar people."[3] What gives rise to this insensitivity on the part of the upper classes to the fate of the lower classes, which so shocks us democratic men?

In effect, in our societies, "all men have just about the same way of thinking and feeling. Each of them can judge in an instant the feelings of all the others. He casts a rapid glance on himself and that is enough."[4] Each person immediately transports himself, by imagination, into the suffering body of his fellow man because he senses the different positions that individuals occupy as something "accidental"[5] and spontaneously conceives that he could find himself in the place of the other. In these societies, imagination causes one person to identify with another with a force that breaks down barriers of class and those barriers that give rise to war itself. "The question of foreigners or enemies has no bearing. Imagination immediately puts them in their place. It mixes something personal with its pity."[6] This pity is not disinterested. It is because I imagine myself in the place of a suffering other that I am interested in his fate. But at the same time, the result of this imaginary identification is that I voluntarily take it upon myself to lighten his fate.

That to which pity engaged me is not in fact the other nor, by a trick of the imagination, me. It is what is similar in me and the other that I am concerned about. This play of the imagination does not give me access to the other as such, nor does it leave me confused as to the limits of myself. It concerns and opens to a *tertium quid* which is what Tocqueville calls the *semblable* ("one's likeness").

We have seen in the preceding chapter how the intelligence of democratic man spontaneously generalizes all ideas and impetuously rushes to abstraction. We now see another aspect of the same process, which concerns the emotion. This *semblable* that democratic man wishes to comprehend by the most general and inclusive of ideas possible is intimately linked to him by pity, which identified democratic man with each and every one of his fellows. The generalizing abstraction and the identifying emotion obey the same impulse. Through the general idea, he identifies each man with every other man. Through an active pity, he identifies himself with any other individual whatever. In this double process, intellectual and emotional, democratic man neither affirms himself as a self nor forgets himself in the other.

The self and the other come together differently in aristocratic societies. "The same aristocratic institution which made beings belonging to the same species so different did however unite one to another by very tight political ties."[7] Certain individuals belonging to one class were strongly linked to others belonging to another class. As we have seen in Chapter Three, it is because the servant is so *different* from the master that the latter ends up regarding him as a subordinate part of himself, prolonging and extending his own being. For his part, the servant is able to identify himself so completely with the master as to "end up disinterested in his very self."[8] It is because the social conditions are extremely different that the affirmation of self, like devotion to another, can manifest itself so completely. "Men who live in aristocratic centuries are therefore almost always bound tightly to something placed outside them and are often disposed to forget themselves."[9] Thus, in aristocratic societies, the affirmation of self and self-forgetting are reciprocally conditioned, apportioned as they are between two socially distinct classes. The rigid social division forces each to recognize the existence of the *other*. In democracies, on the other hand, where each never ceases wanting to identify himself with the other and the other with his self, the self and the other are simultaneously eroded. The inevitable presence of the other explains the harshness of aristocratic societies, while in democratic societies, the simultaneous erosion of the affirmation of self and the recognition of the other produces this third element, the *semblable*, an abstract middle term appropriate to the gentleness that is characteristic of these societies.

The increasing gentleness in democratic societies not only characterizes relations of individuals among themselves, but also the relation of political power with individuals. In both cases, the effects of this progress are equivocal. Consider, for example, Chapter Seven of part one of volume I of *Democracy* which covers "*Of Judicial Discretion in the United States.*" Here, as always, Tocqueville carries out a comparison with what happens in Europe.

> Judicial discretion in the United States only indirectly undermines the principle of the division of powers. It does not threaten the existence of citizens. Judicial power does not, as in Europe, hover over the heads of everyone, because it applies only to those who, in accepting public office, have submitted in advance to its requirements. It is at one and the same time less fearsome and less effective.[10]

Fortunately, American judicial discretion differs from judicial discretion in Europe in its greater respect for constitutional rules and individual rights. For these very reasons, American legislators have made recourse to the judiciary "a common instrument" of government. Tocqueville writes: "From this perspective, it exerts perhaps more real influence on the social body in America than in Europe. However, one must not be taken in by the apparent mildness of American legislation in what concerns judicial matters."[11] If judicial decision-making in the United States is less fearsome, its mildness is nevertheless misleading. Because the body that pronounces these judgments obeys the same influence as the body that brings charges, there is little chance of being acquitted by it. "Condemnation is less to be feared but it is more certain."[12] Thus, the constant pressure of an influence that proceeds with a relative mildness is stronger than the great, and therefore rare, authoritative blows that cause one to tremble. Tocqueville continues: "nothing is more frightening than the wave of American laws when they define political crimes, properly understood. . . . But what in this makes American laws so fearsome is born, if I may dare say, of that very mildness."[13] Thus, in less than a page, the landscape that Tocqueville describes changes from top to bottom. Judicial power in the United States was first esteemed to be less fearsome and less effective than in Europe. However, no contradiction exists between the two appraisals, because Tocqueville shows how, by virtue of its very mildness, judicial power is more frequently employed and administered by judges who share the same passions as the prosecutor. One can understand Tocqueville when he declares at the end of this chapter: "And I do not know if on the whole, judicial power, as one understands it in the United States, is not the most formidable weapon that has ever been put into the hands of the majority."[14]

Thus, in democratic societies, social power grows in proportion to the mildness of its procedure. It is the sway of the same idea—the *semblable*—that forbids the use of violence toward another with whom one identifies so easily, and that leads this other ever more completely to submit to the will of the masses, so identified with. Mildness is the balm and the poison of democratic societies.

This mechanism allows us to understand what Tocqueville writes concerning "the kind of despotism that democratic nations have to fear."[15] In the chapter so entitled, the comparison he draws between traditional tyranny and the new "despotism" is carried out according to schema extrapolated from the comparison between political power in the United States and in Europe. Referring to the extreme example of the Roman emperors, he writes: "There tyranny weighed heavily on a few individuals. But it did not extend to the many. It devoted itself mainly to a few grand objectives and neglected the rest. It was violent and narrow."[16] In a similar manner, he describes judicial power in Europe. Immediately after, he envisions democratic despotism: "It seems that if despotism comes to be established among the democratic nations of our time, it would have the following characteristics. It would be more extensive and milder and would degrade men without tormenting

51

them."[17] Ancient despotism was violent and limited; democratic despotism will be "extensive and mild." Democratic man holds torture in horror, but the mild and constant pressure that he exerts over his *semblable*—who is himself—is not less constricting.

Recall the political alternative that Tocqueville places before men who live in a democratic social state: either the sovereignty of the whole or the absolute power of a single individual. All our preceding analysis has described for us and put us on guard against an absolute power, but one emanating from the whole. In fact, what he often appears to describe is a condition of society when this alternative loses its rigidity and where the two terms appear to amalgamate into a "kind of compromise between administrative despotism and the sovereignty of the people."[18] Does Tocqueville come to obscure the distinction between freedom and servitude? God help us! But he is worried. "In vain do you charge the same citizens, which you have made so dependent on the central power, to choose from time to time the representatives of this power. This exercise of their free will, important, but brief and rare, will not prevent them little by little from losing the faculty of thinking, feeling, and acting by themselves and thus gradually falling below the level of humanity."[19] The important thing is this: if nothing authorizes us to blur the distinction between freedom and servitude, the crucial problem of democratic societies then concerns a type of man, a citizen, who will use his constitutional rights and exercise his liberties or who will let himself be deprived of them.

Chapter 6

DEMOCRATIC MAN

Thus, the man of democratic societies, encountering and only wanting to encounter around him equal and similar individuals, does not submit to the influence of others. He searches in himself for his opinions, but he finds them there or recognizes them only if he also sees them in his fellow men, only if they are authorized by common opinion and maintained by all the force of social power. His thoughts readily lead him to abstractions, while his heart willingly opens itself to pity. He is rational, compassionate, and soft. But reasoning and compassion do not occupy his whole life. What does he do in his day-to-day life? What are his principles of action? We have seen that, contrary to the aristocratic man, who is capable of forgetting himself, he never loses himself from view, since he wishes to see everywhere only his own counterpart. What moves this democratic man, Tocqueville tells us, is individualism, which must be distinguished from selfishness.

Selfishness is a passionate and exaggerated love of oneself which brings man to relate everything to himself and to prefer himself to everything. Individualism is a deliberate and peaceful sentiment which disposes each citizen to isolate himself from the mass of his fellow men and withdraw apart with his family and friends. In such a way, after having created a small society for his convenience, he voluntarily abandons society at large to itself.[1]

Individualism is directly linked and intrinsic to the democratic social state in which individuals are independent of one another. It is the reflection and affirmation in the soul of each of this social condition. It is the affirmation by the individual of his self-sufficiency. He does not want to be subjected to the influence of another and does not claim to exercise such influence himself. Individualism is the characteristic of a society where each individual perceives himself as the basic unit of society, similar and equal to all other basic units.

It is self-evident that the dominance of such a perception of the social world attacks public virtues at their source and tends to indefinitely extend the social bond. We have seen that institutions belonging to free societies (in particular, associations) have for their goal the reconstitution of this social bond and the task of reminding democratic men that they live in society. But what are the consequences of such a perception on individual behavior?

Men in democratic societies, although they may attach themselves to such a segment of common opinion as reflects their own good and do not budge from this, are nevertheless not very prone to a strong personal conviction. The content of the opinion is less important than the fact that it comes from the majority. And in claiming this opinion as his own, the individual is first and foremost exercising his right to have a personal opinion, which democratic doctrine accords him. Democratic man, if he does not willingly change opinion, is very given to doubt. He is motivated more by having an opinion than in having a particular opinion. He holds to the opinion more than to the truth of it. Thus, "amidst the doubt of their opinions, men end up attaching themselves solely to their instincts and material interests, which are more visible, palpable, and permanent by their nature than opinion."[2] Within the inviolable and perfect circle of his self-sufficiency, where the individual wants no foreign interest to penetrate, how could he receive opinions that could sustain his conviction, enthusiasm that would lead him to order his life in accord with them, that is, in accord with something outside him and other than him? To order his life in accord with correct opinion would require him to renounce wanting above all to resemble his fellow men in everything, to place the source of all legitimacy in the masses. What then remains for him to want, if not a comfortable preservation of his body?

The philosophers who have laid down the doctrinal basis of modern democratic society (Hobbes and Locke, in particular) supposed that, in order to deliver man from the evils that belonged to differences of opinion (religious opinions, above all), it was necessary to ground social maxims on a principle that no man could deny, which would escape doubt and contradiction because it would not be based on an opinion of man and the world but a passion, the strongest and most universal passion, the preservation of one's life, and preferably in the most comfortable way possible. Everything takes place as if the democratic man that Tocqueville describes had assimilated wholesale this analysis and reproduced it spontaneously in his innermost character. In any case, he at least manifests what their thought concluded.

This democratic man is therefore prey to the passion of material well-being. Certainly, the love of the goods of the world is not peculiar to the citizens of democracy. But there it takes an intensity and, especially, a completely novel form that forces one to see in it a specific characteristic of these societies. In aristocracies, the search for material goods cannot become the dominant theme of social life, because society is divided between a ruling class that has goods beyond measure and for whom wealth is not "the goal of life" but a "way of life,"[3] and a mass of men who are deprived of goods and are without hope of acquiring them. Society is therefore divided into two groups. One group is too accustomed to the assured presence of material goods, and the other too accustomed to the no less certain absence of goods, so that it is not possible that the seeking of material well-being could ever orient the life of society.

In democratic societies characterized by equality of conditions, these two extreme positions tend to disappear in favor of a mean, in which the desire to acquire and the fear of losing

55

what one has acquired reinforce each other's effects to the point of bringing the democratic soul to an obsessive concern for material goods. However, scenes out of the *Satyricon* are not the upshot of his desire for material pleasure. The democratic public exhibits only moderation in matters of bodily pleasure because it willingly sacrifices the possibility of a great present enjoyment to a future where moderate enjoyment is guaranteed; because one has to be on one's guard not to violate equality too seriously, even in what belongs to the body; because, finally, great individual excesses are rare in a society subject to the domination of the masses. "I reproach equality, not because it leads men to forbidden pleasures, but because it absorbs them entirely in the search of permitted pleasures."[4]

However, anxiety is not absent from this quest for material well-being. If everyone has this goal fixed in his sight, the choice of means still stays open, and this choice entails hesitancy, doubt, and regret. Americans are "incessantly tormented by a vague fear of not having chosen the shortest route to take them there."[5] Tocqueville shows us the American building a house for his advanced years and selling it unfinished, clearing a field and leaving it to others to harvest it, always devoured by an "anxious curiosity."[6] He continually shows him engrossed in "the futile pursuit of total felicity which incessantly flees before him."[7] Thus, one sees Americans continually change their direction "for fear of missing the shortest route that can lead them to happiness."[8]

This anxiety is such that the search for the fastest and surest way to attain perfect well-being attracts them more than this well-being itself. This can be seen in the American way of doing business. The American trader ignores all counsels of European prudence in navigating his ship and inflicts upon himself all forms of privation to go faster than his competitor. "During a crossing of eight or ten months, he has drunk brackish water and lived on salted meat. He has struggled incessantly against the sea, illness, and boredom. But on his return, he can sell a pound of tea for a penny less than the English merchant. He has attained his goal."[9] Where in this account do we find the calm, deliberate enjoyment of bodily pleasures apropos of democratic man? Tocqueville goes so far as to write: "Americans exhibit a kind of heroism in the manner in which they conduct business."[10] The term heroism does not appear by chance, given that Tocqueville wants to draw a parallel between the way Americans conduct business and the way the French conducted war during the Revolution. In both instances, men were asked to make efforts that they had never been asked to make before. They were asked to put their lives at risk in a ready and willing manner.[11] This contradiction in democratic man between his taste for tranquil pleasures and his capacity to forsake comfort and risk his life finds its most succinct and complete expression in his attitude toward war.

Tocqueville's statements to the contrary must be acknowledged, however. "The ever-increasing number of propertied friends of peace, the development of moneyed wealth that war devours so rapidly, those indulgent mores, that softness of heart, that disposition to pity that equality inspires, that coldness which makes men little sensitive to poetic and violent emotions which armed service breeds—all these causes unite to extinguish the military spirit."[12] But he does not conclude that war will henceforth be an anachronism bound to disappear from the life of democratic peoples.[13] Surely, such types will always show a reluctance to engage in war. But once engaged, they know how to conduct it as well and perhaps better than others. The fact is that war fires the ambition of each soldier and produces on the democratic army the same effect that a revolution produces in the populace at large. All the desires of democratic men are distilled and come to blaze forth in the breast of the soldier, for "equality opens ambition to everyone and ambition is prompted to hazard its all in the face of death."[14] In an even more revealing statement, Tocqueville writes that there exists "between military and democratic mores a hidden rapport which war uncovers."[15] He describes this rapport:

Men in democracies naturally have a passionate desire to quickly acquire the goods they covet and to enjoy them in ease. Most of

57

them love risk and fear death much less than pain. It is in this spirit that they come to lead commerce and industry. And this same spirit transposed to the field of battle brings them willingly to expose their lives in order to assure, in a single moment, the prize of victory. There is no grandeur so satisfying to the imagination of democratic people than military grandeur, a brilliant and sudden grandeur that is obtained without work, in only risking one's life.[16]

Thus, Tocqueville, after having attributed to democratic men "a cold reasoning that makes them little sensitive to the poetic and violent emotions which armed service breeds," here discovers a singular affinity of the democratic imagination for military grandeur. Note also that he elsewhere insists on the warrior origin of the European nobility and on the warrior foundations of the aristocratic ethos.[17] But in granting that democratic man has a passionate desire to acquire quickly the goods he covets and to enjoy them in ease, one would think that the far-sighted individualism of this same man would cause him to take into account the incalculable loss that death signifies.

Clearly, it seems difficult to reconcile the different traits of democratic man as Tocqueville fills out his portrait. This man is inclined to peace and to seek material goods. But he is also quite capable of renouncing the smallest comfort if this permits him to sell more cheaply than his competitor and even very disposed to risk his life once war has torn him away from his routines. The question is, how does he reconcile these contradictions while remaining true to democratic principles. We should begin by taking note that the commercial "heroism" of Americans is analyzed by Tocqueville in the last chapter of volume I of *Democracy* in the course of which he studies the qualities "which are American without being democratic."[18] We might conclude that what Tocqueville deduces here is not characteristic of democratic man in general, but things specifically American. This holds true, but as an explanation goes only so far. We should take note that the commercial "heroism" of Americans is depicted against the background of a general characterization of Americans that corresponds to the portraits of democratic man that are found in other chapters of *Democracy*.[19] Moreover, this objection has no validity in matters of war, and it is in the case of war that the paradoxes of democratic man stand out.

We have already given voice to the key word that explains the enigmas of democratic man: anxiety. Uncertain of his place in society now that all ranks are leveled, no longer finding a guide in tradition now that the links of time have been broken, uncertain of his opinions to the extent that he doubts the value of opinion as such, democratic man does not know how to orient his life. Material goods are the sole fixed point, the sole incontestable value amidst the uncertainty of all things. But as the modes of production and acquisition of these goods are defined neither by tradition nor the convictions of the individual, this quest for material goods is unlimited and the means to them perpetually changing. As customs no longer exist, everything is customary; there is no time for things to settle into place as change is constant. As there is no longer any conviction—shared opinion about the world—to guide this quest, his only point of orientation is his competitor. To sell more cheaply is the law for this man without law. As the enjoyment of material goods is finally no more intrinsically satisfying for democratic man than for his predecessor in history, this man is not happy despite having so many reasons for being so, and the motive of his life is diversion.

I have seen in America the freest and most enlightened men, placed in the happiest of circumstances that the world can offer. It seemed that a kind of cloud habitually hung over their heads. They appeared grave and almost sad even in their pleasures. He [the American] will travel five hundred leagues in several days in order to be better distracted from his good fortune. Death finally intervenes and stops him before he is tired of this futile pursuit of total felicity which incessantly flees before him. At first, it is astonishing to contemplate this strange agitation to which so many happy men give witness in the very midst of their abundance. This spectacle, however, is as old as the world. What is new is to see a whole people display it.[20]

The Tocquevillian description of democratic man sometimes appears as a page torn from the *Pensées* of Pascal, dealing with the misery of man. Democratic men are small, but it is a great drama in which they play.

This man experiences the anxiety of one who no longer relies on custom and no longer dares rely on his own reason or that of another. He no longer knows anything but calculation. But there is passion in this calculation, for it orders his life. What relief, then, when war changes the rules of the game and raises its stakes. Democratic men "love chance" because the act of facing it is filled with calculation. On the morning of battle, chances are strictly equal. The sublime bet of war is the consummation of prosaic calculation. "The habits of soul" of democratic men prepare all equally for the risk at hand.[21] In this continual calculation of risks that is war, the individual is deprived of and delivered from the sole point of reference in his day-to-day life—his competitor. Equality of condition is perfectly realized without competition, this motive of anxiety with which he is constantly spurred as a private citizen. War is a remedy to the evils of his condition, and as a remedy is in harmony with this same condition. The fact is that the anxiety of competition is felt still more acutely than the love of material goods. Such anxiety is more constant and deeply felt than the propensity to make war, an event that occurs rarely and contradicts all the tasks of day-to-day life.

The competition of everyone with everyone else is the direct result of equality of conditions. The barriers that separate men are lowered; unlimited possibilities seem to open before each individual. But disillusionment, necessarily, follows quickly. "They have destroyed the privileges that encumber some of their fellow men, and they face competition from everyone. Barriers have not been removed. Rather, they have changed their form."[22] Democratic man no longer has around him any-

one but his *semblables* but these are just so many more com-
petitors in the pursuit of the goods of the world.

Democratic man thus finds himself in a paradoxical situation. On the one hand, he can only see and only wish to see his
semblable around him. On the other hand, he perpetually en-
counters an obstacle insofar as the *semblable* is richer, more enterprising, or is more successful than him. The *semblable* is an
obstacle insofar as he is superior to him, insofar as he remains
distinguished by any sign of inequality. The *semblable* is an obstacle to him insofar as he is not yet completely his double.

In such a situation, two attitudes, two strategies are available
to democratic man. Either he strives to reduce this inequality
by bringing himself to the level of his competitor and, if possible, surpassing him. This is the option of the American businessman. It is an enterprise invested with a certain "heroism."
His other choice is to strive to reduce this inequality by bringing the more fortunate competitor, or whoever has the luck to
be more fortunate, down to his own level. The latter attitude is
the product of an aroused envy. These two attitudes are equally
adapted to the democratic social state. But they are not equally
probable. The social state favors the second over the first. This
is why the exploits of the American businessman are described
in a chapter that covers subjects that are specifically American
and not generally democratic. The businessman's behavior is
conditioned by democracy, expressive of democratic man in a
sense, but it is dominated by envy, in less intimate harmony
than the other.

The American businessman sees in his competitor an equal.
That is why he cannot accept the latter's being richer, more enterprising, or more successful. But he strongly differentiates between himself and his competitor, and this differentiation is the
very thing that conditions a struggle between them. Above all,
he recognizes the objectivity of the market, the rules of the
game. Between these two equals, the rules of competition prevent reciprocal identification, which loosens the hold of the idea
of a "semblable." Accepting these rules presupposes accepting

differences and a certain inequality, "accidental," of course, surely destined to be overcome, but real and legitimate. The strongest tendency of democratic society is an increasing intolerance for this inequality, so forceful is the imperative to reduce each to a "semblable." Democratic society encourages competition among everyone, and it is the very fact of being in competition that the democratic spirit wishes to abolish, since to accept competition is to accept the possibility and legitimacy of a certain inequality.

We can sum up the situation of democratic man as follows. The democratic social state undoes the social bond and places individuals on the same level. Each is considered a basic unit of the social body, equal and similar to every other. It follows that what moves democratic man can be immediately generalized to the whole of the social body. What moves everyone else is immediately believed capable of moving any particular individual. The emotional motive in such a situation is the presumptive identification of each with all and all with each. Everything that prevents or appears to prevent, hinders or appears to hinder, this identification is a source of anxiety. What threatens this identification is inequality and all that calls it to mind or anticipates it. What the individual loves in a given citizen as in the social body as a whole is not this or that quality or opinion, it is the quality or opinion that is also his. It is the *relation* of equality and similarity between him and the other or others. And what he hates is, inversely, the very fact of difference and inequality. What he loves is an abstraction; what he hates is also an abstraction. The democratic social state appears on the emotional and the intellectual levels as love of equality. "The first and most lively of the passions that equality of conditions engenders is the love of this same equality."[23]

Because the object of this passion is an abstraction, a relation, this passion is unlimited. It cannot be satisfied nor the anxiety of democratic man appeased. Once this abstract passion is engaged and instituted, there is no reason for its movement ever to cease. To the contrary: It tends to accelerate. The more equality progresses, the more its weight increases, the more the idea of a "semblable" becomes compelling. And while in the centuries of inequality, the most marked differences of condition were self-evident, in the centuries of equality, the least inequalities are insufferable. "The desire for equality becomes ever more insatiable as equality is more widespread."[24]

Competition among everyone is the natural effect of equality of conditions, but it is intolerable. In effect, individuals have an equal right to participate in the race. But if one at the starting line is richer, better trained, then the competition is not equal. Whatever the level of equality we end up with, we can always say, without risk of being wrong, that the competition isn't "really" equal, and that it is therefore necessary, before giving the signal that starts the race, to bring everyone down to the point of real equality, which will allow us to consider the competition finally as really equal. Moreover, it is the very idea of competition that tends to render all inequality intolerable. If social life is presented as a competition between supposedly free individuals, the least superiority held by one member of society appears as an unjustifiable privilege. The principle of competition, when it tends to reign alone in a society, is self-destructive. If existing inequalities are not justified or accepted by virtue of another principle, the very idea of equal competition requires that they be abolished.

Finally, the process of prescriptive identification suffers from an intrinsic weakness. As similar to one person as another may wish, think, and experience himself to be, as obvious as the signs of this similarity may be, the fact remains that two similar individuals remain two distinct individuals. The one is not the other. The identification of each with the other can never be complete. Or rather, only one means exists to overcome this final and apparently unsurpassable otherness. That means is, to conceive and construct, between and above individuals, a third thing whose mission and reason for existence is to realize, guarantee, and symbolize this equality and resemblance—the *central* power. I can identify myself with it and identify the other in it since this third thing is not a distinct individual, and because the individuals, distinct from me, who occupy this

63

place of power, are not in any way perceived in the manner that those I perceive around me in society are perceived. They are not the object of my passion for equality, but its *instrument*. "The sovereign, necessarily and indisputably above all citizens, does not excite anyone's envy, and each believes he takes from his equals all the prerogatives he concedes to it."[25] Democratic citizens, who can never identify completely with one another, can identify completely with the central power, and "they believe that they accord to themselves everything which they give" to this power.[26]

We find ourselves here at the heart of the Tocquevillian vision in its richest and most original expression. The depiction of the passion for equality gives *Democracy in America* its truest color. The problem of democracy is the problem of democratic man, and the defining characteristic of this man is the passion for equality. This is what brings together an unprecedented mix of prosaic calculation and unlimited anxiety in the same person. This is what brings together tranquil well-being and "this immortal and more-and-more intense hatred of the least privilege."[27] Faced with these effects, Tocqueville simultaneously exhibits an ironic condescension and a frightened fascination and mixes in the same sentence indulgent and friendly irony with Pascalian trembling.

In a very real sense, democratic man is a new man. When equality ceases to be either a formal requirement for communitative justice or a synonym for all men belonging to the same species or having their equal dignity before God, when equality becomes the very horizon of social existence and the principle in whose name all is experienced and judged, when the construction of an equal society is the very task that men give themselves, the nature of man knows a new condition.

This passion for equality has three elements that must be differentiated, whose synthesis gives the passion its force and singular scope. The first is universal human sentiment, negatively expressed by envy, and positively expressed by the instinct for justice when justice demands equality. Next is the emotional state peculiar to democratic society. This is the propensity of each to identify with the other and with all, marked by a very lively and constant feeling of the similarity of men. Finally, the third is an intellectual and abstract element that fleshes out the object at which the passions aim. The third element is the most important. It is identical with the fundamental opinion according to which the democratic social body is thought of and perceived. This element is the notion of a social state of nature, constituted by equal and independent individuals such that the society that they are forming could truly be said to be founded on the simultaneous consent and obedience of all.[28] This element is democracy's legitimating principle and animating task. This state of nature is impossible to realize and is unimaginable, but it can be conceived the moment one thinks of nature as equality. At least, it is sufficiently conceivable to be able to be willed. What remains inconceivable in it gives an unlimited field for the will to establish it. If thought cannot come distinctly to conceive the ultimate term of the egalitarian task, it always knows the next step—to reduce the inequalities that are there. That is sufficient for the will.

The reconquest of the state of nature where equality reigns, the establishment of the conditions of perfect competition requires the centralized state to forbid anyone at all from rendering his "semblable" dependent on him or from enjoying an unmerited privilege in competition, which must be kept rigorously equal. In identifying himself with this central state, each can identify himself completely with all the others, for this third—instrument of the end of each and representing the similarity and equality of all—suspends and annuls the separation of similar individuals. It seems that democratic man can hope to rejoin natural equality only at the price and in favor of this enormous artifice.

Chapter 7

DEMOCRACY AND THE NATURE OF MAN

This artifice of the central power, which is the favorite instrument of democratic man, invites us to wonder about the degree to which democratic society is compatible with and completes the nature of man. Is the passion for equality that is the spring of this society compatible with or contrary to the nature of man? What is the fate of "the inequality of intellects" in particular, which "comes directly from God?"

We have seen how democracy tends to abolish the influences of a natural aristocracy of reason and virtue, an abolition that delivers men over to pressures from common opinion and to intellectual laziness. But one could object, if democracy makes it difficult for superior men to act on other men, it does not forbid these superior men from developing their potentialities for themselves, from realizing their natures. This is the very notion that Tocqueville at times seems to doubt when, for example, he studies *"Why Americans are more devoted to Practical Science than Theory."* (Chapter Ten of part one of volume II.) He first asserts that "the pure desire to know" will spring up among Americans, despite the social state that inclines them more toward practice, because it is given to certain individuals by nature. "I do not doubt that there will be born every so often in a few individuals an ardent and inexhaustible love of truth that nourishes itself and is necessarily enjoyed without ever being

67

able to satisfy itself."[1] After a brief portrait of Pascal, as a model of the pure love of truth, he writes the following: "The future will show whether these passions, so rare and so fecund, will be born and be developed as readily in the midst of these democratic societies as in the midst of aristocracies. As for myself, I confess I hardly believe so."[2] The fact is, in aristocracies the class that rules over opinion is naturally encouraged by its position to "conceive very vast ideas of the dignity, power, and grandeur of men."[3] These ideas have a beneficial influence on those who have intellectual tastes, for they "pave the way for the natural impulse of the spirit toward the highest regions of thought and naturally dispose the mind to have before it the sublime and almost divine love of the truth."[4] By placing certain men in a sublime social position, the aristocrats set forth a sublime idea of man, and stimulate in some men (who are not necessarily the same as the first) sublime efforts toward the truth. Aristocracy favors intellectual *eros*. Nothing of the kind takes place in democracies, where nature is left to itself, and where it therefore runs the risk of falling short of its potential.

When Tocqueville contemplates democratic man, the image of Pascal is constantly in mind, and he finds it difficult to think that Pascal could blossom in a democratic social state. It is Pascal whom he brings forth and quotes when he asks himself *"Why One Finds in The United States So Many Ambitious Men and So Few Grand Ambitions."* (Chapter Nineteen of part three of volume II.) "What also prevents men in democratic times from devoting themselves readily to an ambition for great things is the time they see must elapse before they are in a state to undertake them. Pascal said that 'the capacity which allows an eighteen- or twenty-year-old to develop as another would at fifty is a great advantage. It is thirty years painlessly gained.' What takes place there during thirty years ordinarily lies outside the orbit of the ambitions of democracies. Equality which leaves each to his own faculties to arrive at everything retards the process of self-development."[5] This passage is all the more striking because Pascal's words intend to be a satire on the condition of the great, while Tocqueville turns them to the advantage of aristocracy.

It therefore seems that the democratic idea that is "so simple and natural,"[6] corresponding to the "precise" idea of freedom, affirming the equality of men "obviously similar,"[7] puts the nature of man in danger in its most eminent and salient characteristics, of which thought is the most prominent. The preceding chapters and these last remarks lead us to conclude that, in the matter of democracy, it is nature that puts nature in danger. This paradox goes to the heart of the very nature of democracy, in Tocqueville's view. He affirms the two terms with equal insistence. To remain faithful to his thought, this double affirmation has to be respected.

That democracy conforms with the nature of man can not be doubted after reading Chapter Eight, part three, volume II, entitled *"The Influence Of Democracy On The Family."* Proceeding as usual, he compares the aristocratic family and the democratic family. In the former, the father exercises a power that could be called political. "The father not only has a right by nature to rule, he has been granted a political right to the same effect. He is the author and support of the family. He is also its magistrate."[8] Moreover, it is in him alone that political power is properly placed. "With men bound to one another, it is enough to direct the first. The rest follow."[9] In the democratic family, the father does not play as eminent a role because "the general idea of superiority becomes weaker and less distinct."[10] Each individual wants to judge for himself, and so the power of the father's opinion lessens. In addition, the way the inheritance is divided puts all members of the family on an equal plane. The upshot is that "the relations between father and son become more intimate and gentle. Rule and authority are met less often there. Confidence and affection are often greater. And it seems that the natural bond tightens while the social bond loosens."[11] The relations among children also change. In the aristocratic family, the right of the eldest assures that the children have a representative to defend their interests in society.

But although their interests often agree, "it is rare that their hearts are in accord."[12] In the democratic family, the way inheritance is divided makes this community of interest less clear, but the intimacy of family life "melds their souls together."[13] A single word captures the character of the democratic family. It is mildness (*douceur*), and it is repeated three times in this short chapter.

We have already heard this as a leitmotif of democratic societies.[14] But the Tocquevillian analysis of the mildness (*douceur*) that reigns among citizens and between the state and citizens leaves one with an ambiguous impression. Among citizens, it is expressed by service to one another and a tendency toward compassion. However, the easy identification of one individual with another does not allow for great devotions and does not contradict the basic individualism of these societies. In relations between the state and citizens, *things* are equivocal. Mildness becomes frankly menacing. The terrible mildness of judicial power in the United States is the most effective instrument of democratic despotism. Here, in the setting of the family, nothing comparable holds. Certainly, mildness here is always irresistibly charming. "The mildness of these democratic mores is so great there that the partisans of aristocracy themselves are taken in by it. After having tasted it for some time, they are not tempted to return to the respectful and cold formalities of the aristocratic family."[15] But this mildness is not the facade of a more menacing power. It is the mildness of nature itself. All the mockery and irony that often accompany Tocqueville's description of democratic man are forgotten. This idyllic description of the democratic family is redolent of a Rousseauistic perfume. The mocking irony turns against the enemies of democracy. "I have seen ardent enemies of democracy who insist on being "addressed in the familiar 'tu' form by their children."[16] One cannot resist democracy because one cannot resist nature. The family is the privileged place where the general truth about democracy is revealed. "What I have just said about filial love and fraternal tendencies must be understood to apply to all passions that have as their source nature itself."[17]

It follows that the sentiments and passions created by the aristocratic social bond, whose force and grandeur Tocqueville often celebrates, are revealed for what they are: *conventions.* The proof is that the bond does not survive the disappearance of aristocratic society. "There was nothing more tightly bound than the knot that tied vassal to lord in the feudal world. Now these two men no longer know each other. The fear, recognition, and love that formerly tied them have disappeared. Their traces cannot be found."[18] It is impossible to recreate this link because it has no origin in nature. What democracy destroys, and what was aristocracy's grandeur, is ultimately only convention. "Democracy, which destroys or obscures almost all former social conventions and eases the way to the new, causes the majority of sentiments born of convention to disappear entirely. But it only modifies others, and often gives them an energy and mildness that they didn't have."[19] What democracy destroys leaves the way open to nature in all its force, which is energy and mildness.

Ending this chapter, Tocqueville writes: "I think it not impossible to summarize in a single sentence the whole meaning of this chapter and several others preceding it. Democracy weakens social bonds, but it tightens natural ones. It brings the family together at the same time that it separates citizens."[20] To say that democracy reinforces natural sentiments while it weakens social bonds is clearly to suggest that society is not natural. The Tocquevillian conception of the nature of man incontestably seems very close to that of Rousseau.

Aristocracy is on the side of convention, while democracy is on the side of nature. In other words, aristocracy is on the side of the particular, and democracy on the side of the general or universal. And the more society democratizes, the more it is modeled on what is universally human. This point is elaborated in Chapter Eighteen, part three, volume II, *"Of Honor In The United States And In Democratic Society."* Here is how Tocqueville defines honor: "Honor is nothing but that particular pattern established in a particular state by the aid of which a people or class allocate praise and blame."[21] Therefore, the more the human group becomes particular, the more its notions of honor are simultaneously "precise," "bizarre," and strongly felt. The extreme case of this particularization of honor is found in the feudal aristocracy of Europe. The less a group is closed and particularized, the more its notions of honor are generalized and approach universal notions of good and evil without, however, ever completely melding with them. But at the same time, they are less precise and less strongly felt. Thus, as one passes from an aristocratic society to a democratic one, honor in generalizing itself becomes at the same time truer and less active.

> With aristocratic peoples, all ranks differ from one another, but all of them are fixed. Each person occupies a place that he cannot leave and there he lives, surrounded by others attached around him in the same manner. In these nations, no one can therefore hope or fear not to be seen. He does not meet a man so low that he does not have his own dramatic role to play and who would escape praise and blame by his obscurity. In democratic states, on the contrary, where all citizens blend into the same crowd, agitating incessantly, public opinion can not take hold. Its object disappears each moment and escapes it. Consequently, honor there will always be less imperious and urgent. This is because honor acts itself out only in public view. Thus, it is different in this regard than simple virtue, which takes its bearing from itself and is satisfied by its own witness.[22]

As democratic nations devote themselves to an honor that distinguishes them as nations, patriotism is much livelier than in aristocratic societies. "Honor emanates only from the particular needs of the nation itself. It manifests its individuality among different peoples."[23]

Insofar as nations lose their particularity and become democratic, societies increasingly tend to a more-and-more exact conformity with universal notions of good and evil. Thus, it clearly seems that the human species would soon maintain the same ideals and moral sentiments. Tocqueville clearly envisions such a possibility. "Let us suppose that all races fused together and all the peoples of the world came to the point of having the same interests and needs, and that they no longer differed from one another by any distinguishing trait. In such a case, we could entirely cease attributing conventional value to human actions. Everyone would see things in the same light . . . the general needs of humanity, which conscience revealed to each man, would be the common standard. We would no longer meet anything in the world but the simple and general notions of good and evil which would be naturally and necessarily linked to the ideas of praise and blame."[24] Of course, the tense employed is the conditional. But this hypothesis accords with the constantly increasing resemblance among democratic societies that Tocqueville describes, a resemblance that increases even when nations remain distinct. "Two neighboring peoples could not develop the same democratic states without soon adopting similar opinions and mores because the spirit of democracy causes men to become increasingly similar."[25] Consequently, in spite of the division of a democratic humanity into nations—supposing that this division continues—the members of all the nations would maintain the same ideas of good and evil, the same notion of honor.

Why does Tocqueville stick to the conditional tense? To avoid the arrogance of the prophet? Perhaps. But we have to look for another explanation. In effect, Tocqueville has affirmed that the more honor generalizes and approaches the universal rules of good and evil, the more its hold on the mind of man weakens. It follows that, at the ultimate stage of democratic evolution, honor would be totally authentic but with no power over the mind of man. In place of the honor that "acts only in public view" would be the simple virtue "which looks only to itself and is satisfied with its own witness . . . that conscience reveals to each man." The triumph of nature coincides with the end of all public life. Democratic humanity would be peopled with very preoccupied solitary walkers.

These democratic men, to whom the voice of conscience would so clearly state the universal rules of good and evil, would cease to cohere, to be citizens. We recall that Tocqueville

73

sees the principal danger of democracy in the separation of men. We have seen the principle of this separateness in the idea of freedom, precisely understood, which finds the citizen assimilated to man in general. Here we see it realized in the moral content of democratic life, which is the realization of the universal nature of man. The danger of democracy is its nature, which is nature. Aristocratic society, which is founded on a false idea of freedom, on bizarre notions of honor, which particularizes men, causes them by the same token to live together and exalt the higher parts of the soul. Democratic society, which is founded on the just idea of liberty, whose notions of honor increasingly approximate universal notions of good and evil which "generalize" men, separates men and weakens the higher parts of the soul. The false idea of nature elevates the nature of man and stimulates exalted achievements—in thought and politics, above all. The true idea of nature dulls the nature of man and makes him incapable of exalted enterprises that are proper to his nature—elevated thought, in particular. It seems then that in the Tocquevillian analysis, the idea of nature is somehow divided. This division is his constant frame of reference, but the frame of reference has a different content, depending on whether the analysis bears on aristocratic or democratic society. It is as if there were two radically different and therefore incompatible modalities of human nature.

In the "*General View of The Subject,*" which closes volume II of *Democracy In America* and therefore the entire work, Tocqueville appears to lean toward this position. "They are like two distinct humanities, of which each has its advantages and particular inconveniences, its good and bad things that are peculiar to it. . . . These societies, differing so prodigiously from one another, are not compatible."[26] In these sentences, Tocqueville comes closest to a relativistic vision of human societies. But one must note that the context is exhortative. He is calling upon his contemporaries to make the best of the democratic societies in which they are condemned to live and to cease entertaining vain nostalgia for the old order. This politic aim is logically distinct from the theoretical question bearing on the relation of democracy and aristocracy to the nature of man. Throughout his work, he speaks of man—his thought, his passions, and action—as of something that is surely modified by the social state, democratic or aristocratic, but that is implicitly one. Human nature, implicitly one, is his frame of reference. Tocqueville is not a relativist.

Therefore, we have to say that human nature manifests itself in accordance with two conditions, the aristocratic condition and the democratic condition.

What leaps to eye in the aristocratic condition, what surely indicates that it is founded on a false idea, is the central role of convention, based on birth. Because an individual is born into a particular family belonging to the ruling class, it is presumed that, whatever his talents and in fact well before he has had the occasion to display any talents, that he possesses a legitimate title to govern a faction of his kind or, rather, a faction of fellow citizens who are not his kind, who occupy lower levels of society. Because society recognizes and affirms this convention, the relative positions of its different members are perfectly visible and defined. The social bond therefore, is particularly strong. All individuals are links in a chain, occupying different positions, but equally fixed. In this society, founded on the inequality of classes, social relations are essentially conducted between *individuals.* In the Middle Ages, "each person knew only a particular man whom he was obligated to obey."[27] The conventional foundation of this society makes it eminently public in character. Or rather, the hierarchy of conditions and their rigidity cause each individual to be born and die in the same public space, where he is known by everyone. Society is constituted by grouping myriad public spaces according to a hierarchy. That the basic unit is the family or aristocratic lineage in no way prevents power and the diverse attributes of social life from being appropriated by individuals. Quite the contrary: in general, society has neither the means nor the desire to situate and judge each individual according to his ultimate value, determined at the end of an impartial and exhaustive inquiry. Society situates and evaluates the individual according to an attribute that is not him, although it belongs only to him. Aristocratic society chooses to judge according to family ties: Jacques is the eldest son of Bertrand. This evaluation is purely conventional insofar as it says nothing of this individual's value in himself. But it is socially useful in its reference to a clearly defined fact that is publicly acknowledged. This social signpost designates only one individual—or at least a very restricted group of individuals, that of eldest sons, for example—and thus gives rise to certain assumptions in the neighborhood, which show themselves publicly and are hardly less precise. Conventional definition by lineage designates a precise public identity and embodies a framework of presumption. One does not have the same idea of the eldest son of a noble and valorous lord as of the son of a lackey, although one does not intimately know either. And these presumptive judgments are often revealed to be quite unjust, an injustice that gives rise to democratic protest. Nevertheless, each person retains a public identity and is fixed in a framework of assumptions by which others will judge him. One may "derogate," while another may show "a virtue that one would not have expected from a man born in such a lowly station." Each person makes his appearance in the world preceded by a conventional and public image, a product of the social position that his forefathers have bequeathed him and the good and bad memories they have left behind, which the descendant is charged to appropriate for himself, to embellish or demean. Thus, this convention that each person inherits is made up of an ensemble of conventions that his ancestors, successively, inherited and of modifications that his ancestors introduced in these conventions by their native qualities and faults. In aristocratic societies, the native character of each individual shows itself and acts only in a framework determined by social convention.

These societies are based on the ruling power that a restricted number of families exercises on the rest of the social body, a ruling power that finds its counterpart and parallels in the very manner in which even the lowest levels of society function.[28] Because this power is exercised by one individual over others, social life is made up of a collection of individual actions and influences. Because these societies are extremely inegalitarian, very great personal influences can make themselves felt. Those who enjoy this influence set the tone of society. For this reason, the image and idea of the power of one man over others occupy the imagination of this society. Certainly, this power is primarily that of individuals to whom the social convention grants the right to govern others. But by the same token, this convention sanctions the idea of the power of one man over another, independent of their conventional social positions. The social convention that recognizes great individual influences opens space in which great natural influences, owing to strictly personal talents and merits of individuals, can be exercised. Aristocratic societies fashion a sublime idea of man and thus support the matrix of the idea of individual responsibility. Pascal could very well expostulate *Three Discourses on the Condition of the Great* to invite the "great" to distinguish strictly between their conventional grandeur and their personal merit. His extraordinary precociousness, his intellectual integrity—rooted in his own nature, to be certain—nevertheless found in the aristocratic convention of grandeur and sublimity an appropriately nourishing setting.

The importance of the idea of individual superiority comes from the following consideration. Individuals who, for example, can recognize in some other individual the capacity to penetrate into the nature of things, to look for truth, are thus able to get outside themselves in a way that gives them access to a world beyond the narrow circle circumscribed by their nature and limited experience. Through the mediation of the superior individual, they leave their egos behind and come to encounter things in accord with the directions he has indicated. To recognize the genius (in the full sense of the term) of Pascal surely does not require us to agree that he is right. It is to feel the necessity of seriously entertaining the possibility of one's own conversion, and thus, eventually, seriously to spell out reasons why, once thoroughly thought through, one does not convert.

In aristocratic society, the framework that structures conventional influences of individuals nourishes the idea of nonconventional influences, that is to say, individual influences based on natural superiorities. Such influences preserve the idea of a natural order of things external to oneself and to which one does not have access in one's ordinary life. They preserve the idea of an objective order; they nourish intellectual *eros*.

In aristocratic society, convention precedes, hides, and protects nature. In protecting it, aristocratic society allows nature to exercise all its force, where the force exists. Only then is a man in a position to rise above mere convention to higher levels through which men interpret the nature of things. Aristocracy perceives nature as both weak and strong—weak because it must be protected by veils of conventions, strong because it will come to light in spite of conventions. Aristocratic man likes to hide nature and believes that nature likes to be hidden.

Democratic man treats the strengths and weaknesses of nature in a different way. Simultaneously, he thinks it stronger and weaker than does aristocratic man—stronger because it has no need of being protected by convention, weaker because convention can negate or destroy it. He believes that it does not like to be hidden, that it asks only to be revealed, that the good will of men to renounce the conventions that obscure it is sufficient to achieve this.

Nature is easily accessible because it is found fully revealed in each man, and this is what makes him similar to every other man. Because nature is fully revealed in each man, nature separates men. What is natural is found in each individual, not in the bond that ties each individual to another. The social bonds can be said to be natural only in family and communal associations.[29] Other social bonds must be secured by artifice and convention.[30]

Democracy supposes men equal and knows that they are not. Tocqueville puts particular emphasis on intellectual inequality, "which comes directly from God." Conventional equality conforms with nature insofar as no man, by nature, has the right to rule over his fellow man. But this convention in no way theoretically dismisses natural inequalities. It only requires that they do not issue into individual influences that subject the weakest to the power of one who is more endowed by nature. Democracy strives to prevent—or at least weaken as far as possible—any influence from an individual, even based on reason or virtue, that subjects the weakest to the naturally better endowed. This done, it supposes that any man at all can fulfill his nature without the help of these influences, which, in any case, are accidental and provisional at most. Democracy tends to impose a real equality of men that it does not uphold in theory. For all that, it tends to stultify human nature. Democracy embodies nature in a way that puts nature in danger.

Aristocratic convention is more visibly distant from nature, more manifestly conventional. The dullest of minds can easily see that going through the trouble to be born is not a very great exploit. But sanctioning the legitimacy of the power of one man over another confirms the reality and power of nature. Democratic convention is most manifestly close to nature. In a sense, it is only another expression for the idea of men belonging to the same species. But by requiring men to relate to each other according to equality, the democratic convention leads individuals to veil in themselves and ignore in another all the sentiments, qualities, and actions that tend to contradict this equality. But nature does not cease furnishing instances of inequality. Without explicitly denying this inequality, indeed even granting its due in theory, democratic convention is constantly preoccupied with organizing men so that they are unconscious of this inequality in their relations.

Aristocratic convention requires public recognition. But this recognition is based on a singular convention. It thus demands a certain reserve on the part of nature.[31] Yet in supporting the idea of individual superiority, the aristocratic convention affirms the superiority of nature over convention. On the other hand, by refusing the idea of an individual superiority that justifies the power of one person over another, the democratic convention must struggle against the very idea of individual superiority and always confine the power of nature more narrowly. It gives itself an endless task. It must prevent nature from not manifesting individual superiority, because this would sanction

79

the idea of superiority in a way that would soon favor the flowering of aristocratic conventions. For nature to be true to itself, the democratic convention must domesticate nature.

The aristocratic convention requires individuals to respect it. The constraints implied by this respect present obstacles to the development of certain individual natures. But it respects the power of nature itself. The democratic convention, on the other hand, requires the obedience of nature itself, all the while assuring each individual and his nature of its respect.

Because the democratic convention is less conventional than the aristocratic convention, closer to nature, its recognition requires endlessly working upon nature itself. Looking to what is equal, the same or similar in man, it penetrates nature and acts on it more profoundly than aristocratic convention. It modifies nature more. It finds an aliment in each social relation. Democratic men can hold convention in respect by holding themselves to respect it, as aristocratic men so respect it.

Aristocratic inequality is concrete, incarnated in certain individuals or families. It is easy to hold it at a distance, at least mentally, since it resides entirely in relations outside oneself. Democratic equality is abstract insofar as it must regulate all the relations among individuals. It is not incarnated in individuals or families but defines a relation between individuals. To the extent that what this convention points to and aims at cannot be concretized, it appears perpetually menaced and contradicted by reality. Individuals who relate to one another according to democratic convention thus find themselves under siege from an abstract passion, the passion for equality. This passion has its origin in nature, since by nature men belong to the same species. But it has no limit in nature, because nature constantly furnishes aliments to nourish it in producing inequalities.

Democratic convention, realizing that aristocratic convention always uses natural superiority as a rationale or pretext to justify conventional superiorities, gives itself as a task to differentiate rigorously between the equal and the unequal in a way that takes away any pretext of favoring aristocratic convention. Once the equality of all that can be—and thus are— equal has been realized and made manifest, existing and future inequalities can be judged legitimate, having their source in nature, not convention. Until that day, all inequalities are legitimately suspect. As this day approaches, and each passing day brings it closer, each surviving inequality provokes an evergreater impatience. The hunger for equality grows as the stock of inequalities diminishes. It is only when nature has been completely subjected to the conventions of equality, when, therefore, it no longer produces inequality, that natural inequalities will finally be authorized to develop freely.

Democracy wishes to fulfill nature. To do this, it takes upon itself to domesticate and subject it. Once this domestication is complete, nature will be itself and nothing but itself. This domestication will never be achieved, because nature produces inequalities. This impossibility, which reveals the contradiction in democracy, is fortunate. The moment this domestication was complete, man would be dehumanized. On the one hand, democracy's project is unrealizable, because it is contrary to nature. On the other, it is impossible to stop short of this democracy and go back to aristocracy. This is because democratic equality also conforms to nature. It follows that we can only moderate democracy; we cannot stop short of democracy, because it fulfills nature. We cannot attain the end of this movement, for it would mean subjecting nature completely and dehumanizing man. We cannot escape democracy. We can never make democracy completely "real," and we must not try. We can and must moderate democracy, limit it, temper its hostility to nature, all the while benefiting from its conformity to nature. To affirm and will democracy insofar as it is in conformity with nature, to limit it insofar as it is contrary to it, such is the sovereign art on which depend the prosperity and morality of democracies.

Chapter 8

DEMOCRACY AND RELIGION

It is in the family that democracy pleads its case most eloquently, that it reveals its happy conformity with the nature of man. It there gives scope to sentiments whose "energy" and "mildness" cause its most ferocious enemies to succumb. It is also in the family that democracy, in America, finds a moderating principle. If the mildness of democracy is revealed in the relation of parents to children, the moderating principle resides in the divergent roles of men and women.

This subject is of the highest importance in the eyes of Tocqueville for "it is the woman who fashions mores."[1] He devotes four chapters to it in volume II, which he makes a eulogy to the American woman. First, he describes a young girl, enlightened and free,who looks at marriage only with circumspection and only after her reason is exercised and matured. Once the step has been taken, she is a spouse who is virtuous, energetic, indomitable. She is, in addition, subject to the control of a public opinion that is particularly severe. But what is most admirable in the American way of life on this point is not the austere family virtue whose motives are not all so elevated,[2] it is that the Americans know how to rigorously differentiate masculine and feminine roles. "America is the only country in the world where constant care has been taken to draw out two modes of conduct for the two sexes, where it is found desirable for the two to walk apace but always in different paths."[3] This division of roles is particularly judicious, since it is inscribed in

83

nature. Certain Europeans, Tocqueville tells us, refuse to recognize this natural difference. Odious consequences will come of it. "One can easily see that in striving to equalize the sexes, both are degraded. And that from this crude melange of the works of nature can come only weak men and dishonest women."⁴ The Americans, on the other hand, have firmly maintained a masculine primacy that is not in contradiction with the fundamental equality of the sexes. "Never have Americans imagined that the consequences of democratic principles could controvert marital power and introduce a confusion of authority in the family. They thought that every association, to be efficient, must have a leader, and that the natural leader of the conjugal association was the man."⁵

Thus, Tocqueville does not think that democratic principles necessarily force us to consider the division of sexual roles, with male primacy, as a convention inherited from aristocratic ages. "Marital power" is authorized by democracy because it has a natural ground. Democratic equality finds there one of its limits.

Tocqueville extols the prudence of Americans "for having admirably understood the true notion of democratic progress."⁶ They are prudent because they have respected nature. But would nature have the strength to make itself respected in the absence of this prudence? Would it have, in this matter, the strength to resist the pressure of equality after having yielded in all others?

By the end of the nineteenth century, the barrier that divided the sexes had yielded.⁷ Are we to think that imprudent Europeans who shamelessly suggested the "crude melange of the works of nature" more exactly foreshadowed the future of democracy than the sage and austere Americans?

In any case, the judicious distribution of the masculine and feminine roles in the United States proves, in Tocqueville's eyes, that it is possible to adapt intelligently to the new conditions necessarily created by democratic equality. The whole Tocquevillian description of the functioning of American democracy reveals a duality, a polarity between what depends on the *instinct*[8] of democracy and what depends on its intelligence. We have already analyzed the central role of the distinction between the "natural effects of the social state" and the democratic political art.[9] This is the great lesson of Tocqueville's American voyage: "Americans have shown that it is not necessary to despair of regulating democracy with the aid of laws and mores."[10]

But where do those who wish to regulate democracy find their rules? The ultimate fate of the judicious distinction of masculine and feminine roles in America forces us to raise this question. In the name of what conception of human nature, of good and evil, of the appropriate and prudent, would they moderate the excesses of democratic equality? In what mental and moral universe would they find their inspiration? Surely not in the democratic convention, in the idea of the sovereignty of the people, precisely whose effects they must moderate.

The model of these moderators is found in the Federalists, whose prudence did so much to assure a stable foundation for the American republic. But because they were at least partially inspired by aristocratic principles, because they "struggled against the irresistible inclination of their century and country," they were destined to succumb to a democratic age.[11] Can democracy only assure its benefits to men by making use of the instruments and prudence of the derisory residues of aristocracy that persist in its midst—issued from a social climate that is radically foreign—only to reject them afterwards or assimilate them as quickly as possible? And when even these propitious ruins, these fertile vestiges remain no longer, then will democracy need them most.

Given democracy's constant and ever-more complete eradication of aristocracy, its progressive distancing from all the influences emanating from the natural superiorities of reason and virtue, its constant and ever-more rigorous domestication of human nature, from where will democracy draw the resources of reason and prudence that will rule its instincts? Since it subjects the whole human world to its laws, these rules can come only from outside this world. Only religion can really moderate democracy.

We have not yet focused on the Tocquevillian analysis of the relation of democracy to religion per se.[12] Yet an exact understanding of their relation is, in his eyes, of the highest importance. The fact is that religion, essential to the prospects of democracy, concerns matters outside of its definition and its nature. Religion is to democracy as the bridle is to the horse. It serves to guide and moderate. Religion lies outside democracy and is its limit.

We have seen that it is as inevitable as it is desirable that men have "dogmatic beliefs."[13] "Among all dogmatic beliefs, the most desirable seem to me to be dogmatic beliefs in matters of religion."[14] The fact is that all the maxims that inspire the actions of men are ultimately founded on "a very general idea that men have conceived of God, of his relations with humankind, of the nature of the soul, and of their duties to their fellow men."[15] Unfortunately, this subject, the most important of all, concerns "ideas" that are "the most difficult for each, left to himself, and by the effort of his reason alone, to bring to a conclusion."[16] It follows that if dogmatic beliefs weaken, men will forever abandon the paths that lead their minds in this direction. "When religion is destroyed in a people, doubt seizes the highest realms of intelligence and half-paralyzes all others. Each becomes accustomed to having only confused and changing notions on the matters that most interest his fellow man and himself. The opinions he has are poorly defended or abandoned. And as one despairs of being able to resolve alone the greatest problems that human destiny presents, one is reduced by self-indulgence to not thinking of them. Such a state cannot avoid enervating souls. It relaxes the springs of the will, and it prepares citizens for servitude."[17]

To fulfill their task in a manly and dignified manner, men need knowledge or opinion of the Whole that includes them and lies beyond. The immense majority of men cannot form such an opinion out of the resources of their own reason. They must therefore receive it on the basis of authority, as a religious dogma. What is more, if we keep in mind that the citizens of democracies have "very dangerous instincts"[18] that lead them to isolate themselves from one another and to pursue material pleasures with an immoderate love, we could conclude that religion, which steers the heart of man in an opposite direction, is even more necessary to them than to other men. Such are the arguments for the general utility of religion and its particular necessity for democratic societies.

In the Tocquevillian analysis, the social utility of religion is largely independent of its intrinsic truth. "Society has nothing to fear or hope from an afterlife, and what is most important is not so much that all citizens profess the true religion but that they profess a religion."[19] It follows that doctrinal differences among the religions, when all are equally authorized, do not detract from their social benefits, especially when, as in the United States, they "preach the same morality."[20] Through their moral teachings, they provide citizens with schooling in mores, more than in beliefs. Religions moderate the ardor to enrich oneself and reign sovereign, especially in the soul of the woman, who determine mores. It should be noted that religion in the United States essentially acts through the intercession of the woman; it finds its support in the only difference—that between men and women—that the American democratic convention still recognizes as founded in nature.

In regulating the family religion indirectly but powerfully helps to regulate society and the state. To determine its relation with these things, it is necessary to see further than its utility, than its irreplaceable ability to fix the opinion of men on the most important subjects. It is necessary to lay out what the particular nature of religion consists in.

Religion or the need of religion is inscribed in the nature of man. There is in each man a disproportion between his aspirations and his life that necessarily engenders the want and hope of another world. "Religion is therefore only one particular form of hope, and it is as natural to the human heart as hope itself."[21] It follows that atheism and religious indifference are contrary to the nature of man. "It is through a kind of aberration of the intelligence and by dint of a sort of moral violence exercised on their own nature that men separate themselves from religious beliefs. An irresistible inclination leads them back to Him. Nonbelief is an accident. Faith alone is the permanent state of mankind."[22]

These assertions provide the key to what must be the relation between religion and political institutions. They tell us, in effect, that religion is strong by itself since, in every man, everywhere and always, it finds a grounding and nourishment in his nature. Thus, it does not need the help of human conventions to make its voice heard and its influences felt. In particular, it does not need the support of political institutions. Quite the contrary: to mix it with political institutions and passions is to weaken it, for this links its destiny to what is by nature destined to obsolescence. "One has never seen a government that finds support in an invariable disposition of the human heart, nor that is grounded in an eternal interest."[23] But religion, in contrast, "finds support only in the sentiments that are the consolation of all miseries" and that thus "can draw to it the heart of humankind."[24]

Therefore to want to aid religion by fusing it to the political order is in reality to weaken it, especially in democratic centuries when political institutions are so fragile and subject to such frequent changes. In order to give religion its full force, it is necessary to leave it to its own force alone. In preserving its purity, one assures it its greatest social utility. "The religion that, as with the Americans, never mixes directly with the government of society must therefore be considered as their premier political institution. If it does not give them a taste for freedom, it facilitates its practice for them in a unique way."[25] Independent of the state, not mixing in its affairs, religion nourishes the soul of the woman, regulates family mores, and determines the moral world.

In determining the moral world, religion guards against the temptation to make bad use of freedom, either through excess or deficiency. In effect, the idea that democracy engenders the total freedom of the individual to decide his destiny can lead to

two opposite but equally deadly consequences. The first is to totally renounce this very freedom, too great for an ordinary individual to know how to use. "When authority no longer exists
in matters of religion, nor in political matters, men soon take
fright at the appearance of this limitless independence. This
perpetual agitation of all things disquiets and tires them. Since
all moves in the mental world, they at least want all to be firm
and stable in the material world and, not being able to resume
their former beliefs, they give themselves a master."[26] The second, the inverse, is audaciously to push things to the point of
affirming that either the individual or society has the right to
do everything by virtue of this unlimited freedom. The tendency of democratic society is to attribute this unlimited right
to society. But religion restrains the American from advancing
such an impiety. "At the same time that the law permits the
American people to do everything, religion prevents them from
thinking that anything goes and forbids it to dare everything."[27]

Thus, in the United States, there is an harmonious marriage
between religion and democratic freedom. Tocqueville sees exemplified there what he calls *"the natural state* of men in the
matter of religion"[28] in the modern age, contrary to Europe and
France in particular, where religion and political society have
no natural rapport. What characterizes the modern situation
with regard to religion is the progress of "indifference" and
"negative doctrines," not so much following an attentive examination of the problem but not even being aware the problem exists, modern men let themselves be led by the current of
ideas of the time. Certainly, such a society will include con-
vinced nonbelievers and believing zealots. But what is decisive
is the attitude of someone who doubts, or who is a nonbeliever
by indifference or softness rather than by conviction.

Two cases are presented. Either, as in the United States,
"though ceasing to believe in the truth of religion, the nonbeliever continues to judge it useful" and professes it publicly so
that those who still believe do not hesitate to profess it, without
timidity but also without aggression. In such a way, "they cre-

ate a public opinion in favor of religion."[29] Such is "the natural state of men in matters of religion" in our time. Or else, as in France, those who know only doubt or indifference hasten publicly to abjure the faith of their fathers, thus provoking a reaction on the part of those who have stayed devoted to this faith to include in one hatred all modern ideas and institutions and, in particular, those which favor political freedom. One could not say that a common opinion exists, hostile to religion but rather a war of opinions where each is pushed beyond the "natural limits"[30] of its own sphere through the mixing of religion and politics. It follows that this state is not natural. It is by freeing religion from its political shackles that religion is reestablished in its natural domain, given back to itself, and at the same time made a friend of political freedom.

This "natural state" is a state of opinion in which certain citizens—surely numerous because their attitudes give the religious tone to the whole society—hide their true sentiments or at least let nothing show of their doubts and hesitations. This transformation of religion into common opinion entails a certain hypocrisy that Tocqueville explicitly recognizes. "In the United States, moreover, the sovereign is religious and, consequently, hypocrisy must be commonplace."[31] We have seen, in addition, that in Tocqueville's eyes the hold of religion illustrates the extraordinary power of public opinion in the United States.[32]

The religious situation in American democracy is thus ambiguous. It is universally professed; its precepts are even more observed there than elsewhere. But Americans profess it and accept it less by conviction and love of its truth than by conviction in its utility. "It is also from this point of view (utility) that the inhabitants of the United States themselves come to think of religious beliefs. I do not know if all Americans have faith in their religion, for who can read into the depth of hearts? But I am sure that they believe it necessary to the maintenance of republican institutions. This opinion does not belong to a class of citizens or to a party, but to the entire nation. It is found at all levels."[33]

This observation casts a strange light on the separation of church and state, of religion from politics, recommended by Tocqueville for the good of religion as for the good of democracy and freedom. The basis of his argument is that democracy needs religion because religion keeps it from "doing everything" and that religion is never as beneficial and truly strong as when it is left to its own resources, rooted only in the hope natural to all men. This argument presupposes that the political utility of religion rests on the authentic and purely religious attachment of each man to his religion. This utilitarian assessment is brought by an outside observer who takes into consideration the natural and universal characteristics of men and the needs of society—in particular, democratic society. When this utilitarianism becomes that of the citizens themselves, the argument of the observer, far from being strengthened is to such an extent, undermined. For religion to have its proper force, it is necessary for men to be devoted to it for itself and not for social utility or by love of the political institutions to which it can be fused. Failing this, they link it to political considerations which, according to Tocqueville's thesis, cannot but corrupt and weaken it. The religion of the Americans loses its utility proportional to their attachment to it for reasons of utility. Such is the central difficulty of the Tocquevillian interpretation of the relation of democracy and religion.

To consider religions exclusively or principally from the point of view of social and political utility is a distinctly ancient point of view. The Western political tradition credits the Roman patrician with enlightened practices in this regard.[34] It has at its basis the idea that nothing is more important for the health of political society than a people disposed to obedience. This disposition to obedience is firmly established only if the people see obligations sanctioned by divine will in the particular rules to which they must conform. Those who govern, the patricians, can snicker among themselves, behind closed doors, about popular beliefs. Out of political prudence they make a duty to scrupulously respect all the rites and precepts of religion in their political comportment. Their hypocrisy is made necessary by the public utility of religion, but this hypocrisy is useful only if it is essentially limited to the ruling class. The point of view of Romans in matter of religion would consider that if disbelief penetrated the ranks of the people, the guarantee of obedience would be undermined, and the body politic would shortly dissolve into anarchy. The men in the popular ranks would in effect be little inclined to a useless hypocrisy.

Tocqueville describes for us a novel device that does not need the precautions of traditional prudence. In the United States, the great mass of men hardly believe, but judge themselves obligated, like the patricians of yore, to save appearances. Each American citizen simultaneously assumes the role of patrician hypocrite and sincere plebeian. He is his own augurer-priest, and that is perhaps why he is so grave. American democracy has democratized the point of view of the Romans in matters of religion. That is why the weakening of religious faith does not issue into anarchy.

However, the bottom line of this democratization seems quite ambiguous, in spite of its remarkable social utility, for the great mass of citizens lose the credit and resourcefulness that came from their sincerity without gaining as compensation the advantages and benefits of intellectual freedom, since, as we have seen in chapter four, there is less true freedom of thought in the United States in matters of religion than in the Spain of the Inquisition. It is very striking that, on the one hand, Tocqueville sees religion as the premier political institution of the Americans, which guarantees and supports freedom in the best fashion, in preventing them from daring all, while preventing them in particular from considering "the impious maxim" . . . "that all is permitted in the interests of society."[35] On the other hand, Tocqueville finds exemplified by the force of this same religion the exceedingly potent social power that democracy asserts over the spirit of men, a social power that is the most implacable enemy of intellectual freedom. Thus, religion forbids Americans, much to their happiness, to conceive the idea of the unlimited power of society only by virtue of the reality of this very power! We might say that in Tocqueville's eyes, religion was

the salutary bridle of democracy. We have to add that the democratic horse has the bit in its teeth.

Christianity is the shared opinion of American democracy.
But this shared opinion is less the instrument of what is properly religious in Christianity than the inverse. Religion is the instrument of this shared opinion, the specific mode of expression
of the social power of democracy. It is not dogma that com-
prises shared opinion; it is shared opinion that is dogma. It follows that the separation of church and state is largely an illusion if one means by this the establishment of their mutual
independence. In the United States, this separation is the vehi-
cle by which the submission of religion to a new political
regime—the democratic regime—is established and expressed.
The point is made clear if we consider the history of American
democracy.

Tocqueville considers that the destiny of the American Republic has been largely determined by the character of its Puritan founding. He readily conceives "the whole destiny of
America contained in the first Puritan who set foot on these
shores, as the whole human race in the first man."[36] What characterizes Puritanism is its mixing of religion and politics. "Puritanism was not only a religious doctrine. It was further amal-
gamated in certain matters with the most absolute democratic
and republican theories."[37] In Chapter Three, part one, volume
I, he summarizes the character of the Puritan founding, and invites his readers to see "the key to almost the whole work."[38]
There, he shows with numerous examples to what degree the
religious commandments were the political law of the society.
"The legislator . . . was above all preoccupied with tending to
the moral order and maintaining the sound mores of society. He
also is incessantly engaged in the domain of conscience, and the
sin almost does not exist that does not end up being submitted
to the censure of the magistrate."[39] Tocqueville summarizes
this thought: "I have already said enough to put the character
of Anglo-American civilization in its true light. It is the product (and its point of departure must constantly be borne in
mind) of two perfectly distinct elements, which elsewhere have

often been at war, but that have come, in America, to be incorporated into a marvelous combination. I mean here *the spirit of religion* and *spirit of freedom.*"[40] Thus, this harmony between religion and the political order, which works to the great benefit of freedom, is revealed in America in two contrary ways: as an inextricable mixture at the time of the Puritan founding and as a strict separation in subsequent American history. What appear to be two opposite phenomena are in no way contradictory. They are two successive phases of the same process.

In Puritan America, in effect, religion ruled over the details of social life. But insofar as the power of religion was exercised by all members of the social body on each and each on all, it could be described not as the power of religion over society but, more judiciously, as that of society over itself by means of religion. Tocqueville shows in detail the degree to which American society takes care of itself and acts on itself, beginning with its Puritan founding. "The law enters into a thousand diverse details to prevent and satisfy a thousand social needs, about which even to this day there is only a confused idea in France."[41] As society progressively tightens its grip upon itself, it has less need of the instrument of religion. The political order progressively disengages itself from the grasp of religion and separates from it. At the same time, the ardent faith of the first Puritans gives way to the grave but superficial respect characteristic of democracy come of age. The less society needs religion to hold together and act upon itself, the more it considers religion as an aspect of its social utility. The extraordinary religious intensity of the first Puritan societies arose because religion still had there the whole strength of faith—a faith that had just escaped persecution. Already, the social power of democracy was manifest. This mixing and amalgamating of the forces of religion and freedom is unique in human history and explains the incomparable founding energy of Anglo-American Puritanism.

In the Tocquevillian description, the character of religion is revealed in a movement between two poles. On the one hand,

94

religion appears from the point of view of universal human nature. apart from and above political vicissitudes. wherein resides eternal human hope. On the other hand. religion appears as shared opinion. particular to this democratic society. which primarily looks to religion for its social utility. One pole is that of natural religion: the other is civil religion. When Tocqueville tells us that to be useful to democracy. religion must be reduced to itself. to its natural. authentic and exclusively religious foundations. and tells us at the same time that American citizens consider it essentially from the point of view of its utility. as shared opinion. the safeguarding convention of the social body. these two assertions can be reconciled in a certain fashion only if natural religion is the civil religion of a particular regime: democracy. Christianity is indeed the premier American political institution. but revealed religion viewed separately as pure natural religion on the one hand and a pure social religion on the other is revealed as the same thing.

Here. we see the American "hypocrisy" in a new light. The democratization of the Roman viewpoint with regard to religion changes in significance. The hypocrisy of the patrician is based on a different interest from that of the people and on the different position he occupies with regard to them. If he were no longer to keep up appearances and. as a consequence. his comportment proved to the people that he no longer believed in the city's religion. the people would no longer hold themselves obedient. But if the American citizen no longer conforms his opinion to shared opinion. is he not rebelling against his own power? The hypocrisy of the patrician veils and protects his power over the people. But what could hypocrisy veil for the American citizen who publicly proclaims. through his political institutions. his own power over the conditions of existence? Tocqueville writes that "religion prevents him from thinking everything and forbids him to dare anything."[42] As far as the American citizen himself considers religion from his first point of view. it becomes clear for us that the American. in professing his religion. "prevents *himself* from thinking everything and forbids *himself* to do anything." By fear or prudence. he recoils

95

before the idea of his absolute self-sufficiency inscribed in democratic principle. Democratic man affirms himself as pure individual freedom that no human or divine authority can obligate without his consent. The Christian religion indeed presents itself as issuing from and guaranteed by divine authority. But democratic man, in professing it and conforming to it for its utility, brings it back into the human sphere determined by his free consent. Since through it he wishes to circumscribe his own freedom, he must define what he has consented to as independent of his consent and inscribed in the nature of man. The democratic citizen is not a religious man. But to appreciate—without his head swimming—this unlimited freedom, which makes him a sovereign individual, he turns schizophrenic and conceives of himself in the image of man naturally subject to God. The American religion is the sigh of the democratic citizen, oppressed by an excess of freedom.

Thus, in America, religion and democracy adapt to one another by changing one another. Democracy willingly stops short of the absolute human sovereignty that its principles postulate. Religion, revealed dogma, tends to turn itself into common opinion, a convention that safeguards society, all the while thinking of itself as a natural religion. In this unequal compromise, Tocqueville sees the natural state of democratic man in matters of religion. Whatever the merits of this device, why does he see in it a "natural state"? Why does not the head-on clash between religion and the new society, which prevails in France, speak more to the truth of these two protagonists? In *Democracy in America*, the French case is only alluded to. To study it seriously, it is necessary to turn to *The Old Regime and the French Revolution*.

Far from veiling the reality of this clash, Tocqueville opens his examination of the study of the essence of the French Revolution (Chapters Two and Three of book 1) with the following remark. "One of the first steps of the French Revolution had been to attack the Church, and, among the passions that were born of the Revolution, the first to be kindled and the last to be extinguished was the passion of irreligion."[43] But although he

96

recognizes the central character of this opposition in the consciousness of the actors, he maintains that "the war against religion was only incidental to this great Revolution and not its
own genius."[44] Why was this only "incidental," a misunder-
standing, as it were? "It was indeed less as a religious doctrine
than as a political institution that Christianity sparked these fu-
rious hatreds, not because the priests claimed to rule over oth-
erworldly affairs, but because they were landowners, lords,
tithe recipients, administrators in this world."[45] The argument
is simple. Because of circumstances that evolved over a long
history, the Christian religion found itself inextricably bound to
a society with which it shared nothing essential. The men of the
Revolution wanted to pulverize this society. Consequently, they
felt a radical hostility toward religion. These reflections presuppose a distinction in right or nature between the political
and religious order, a distinction inscribed in the nature of man
but obscured in particular situations.

The subsequent chapter is entitled: *"How the French Revolution Had Been a Political Revolution That Proceeded in the
Manner of Religious Revolutions, And Why."* Thus, it seems that
a certain mixing of religion and politics is found not only in the
case of the enemy of the Revolution but also took place in some
fashion within the Revolution itself, in the specific way it
evolved. The French Revolution took on an intolerant character. What distinguishes the French Revolution from all preceding political revolutions, which aligns it with religious revolutions, is that it "had no particular territory,"[46] addressing itself
not to citizens of a given country but to all men as men. Christianity, as distinct from pagan religions that "guarded certain
national and often municipal features even in their dogmas,"[47]
considered man in himself, and drew its essentials from human
nature itself, and consequently could equally be received by all
men and applied everywhere. Likewise with the French Revolution: "It was by always going back in this way to what was
least particular and, so to speak, most *natural* concerning the
social state and government, that it would make itself understood by all and be imitated in a hundred places at the same

time."[48] The common point between Christianity and the French Revolution was the universality of their appeal. "The French Revolution had acted with regard to this world exactly in the same manner as religious revolutions act in view of the other."[49] At the end of these opening remarks of *The Old Regime*, Tocqueville's position could be summarized in the following way. Christianity and the French Revolution formally resemble each other by the universality of their appeal, while they differ concretely by the object of their appeal. The difference is infinitely more important than the resemblance, for it is what separated this world from the other world. We are now in a position to understand better how these two great forces could find themselves in competition and conflict and why this conflict is not inscribed in the nature of things, but is contrary to it.

A doubt persists, however. Political revolutions prior to the French Revolution had a field of exercise and an area of legitimacy restricted to a particular group. The field of exercise and area of legitimacy for the French Revolution was nothing more nor less than humanity itself. Does not this extension of the competence of the political order presuppose a change in the understanding of politics that would risk undermining the distinction between the two worlds? By making the *orbis terrarum* the horizon of the revolutionary enterprise, does it not mean invading the territory that until now was peculiar to the Christian religion where it reserved all to itself while leaving to particular political societies the care of its particular affairs.

Tocqueville takes the problem up again and deepens his treatment in the last part of Chapter Two, *"How Irreligion Became a General and Dominant Passion Among the French of the Eighteenth Century and What Sort of Influence That Had on the French Revolution."* He begins by reintroducing his customary themes. Religion is natural to man. Irreligion therefore can not become the general passion of the French, except in consequence of "very particular" causes. Because religion is on the side of the natural and universal, these very particular causes could arise only from the state of society at that time. It is thus necessary to understand "how it [the Church] stood in

98

the way of the political revolution that was brewing."[50] Here is the response. "By the very principles of its government, the Church stood in the way of those whom they [the writers who championed reform] wanted to prevail in the civil government. It relied mainly on tradition, while they professed a great scorn for all institutions that were founded on respect for the past. It recognized an authority superior to individual reason, while they appealed to reason alone. It was founded on a hierarchical organization, while they tended to blur ranks. In order to get along with it, it was necessary for both sides to recognize that political and religious society, being by nature essentially different, could not be ruled by similar principles. But things were quite far from this at the time. It seemed that to attack the institutions of the state, it was necessary to destroy those of the Church, which served then as a foundation and a model."[51] While Tocqueville is apparently elaborating the theme of Chapter Two, book I, we find a radical modification of the argument. It is no longer a question of peculiar political circumstances that define the Church's situation, it is not the "tithe holding curates" who are the targets of the revolutionaries, it is the very principles of the Church as a religious society. Surely, the hinge of his argument, namely the distinction between religion and politics, remains formally intact. However, insofar as one or the other addresses itself to the same man, or one or the other constitutes societies, each citizen sees himself presented with radically opposed maxims, which, commensurate with their generality and comprehensive ambitions, naturally tend to seep out of their original domains and into the other. This is exactly Tocqueville's perspective, because he notes that the institution of the Church set down "the foundation and model" of the political institution of the *ancien régime*. Consequently, the Church does not appear to have been the victim here only of accidental meddling in political affairs without any natural connection to it, but rather to have constituted the paradigm for the political order detested by the revolutionaries. Certainly such an interpretation does more justice to the force of the antireligious passion of the eighteenth century. But it makes it that much more difficult to entertain the possibility of bringing about the harmonious coexistence between a religious society and a political society, founded on radically opposed principles.

Tocqueville himself in *Democracy in America* leads us strongly to doubt this possibility.

> Alongside each religion is found a political opinion that, by a certain affinity, is joined to it. Let the human spirit follow its tendency and it will regulate in a uniform manner the political society and the divine city. It will seek, if I dare say so, to *harmonize* the earth with heaven. The greater part of English America was peopled by men who withdrew from the authority of the Pope and submitted to no religious authority. They therefore brought to the New World a Christianity that I don't know how better to portray than by calling it democratic and republican. This uniquely favored the establishment of a republic and a democracy in public affairs. At the time this principle was established, politics and religion found themselves in accord, and they have not ceased to be since.[52]

Thus, to obey contradictory principles in political society and religious society is contrary to the natural tendency of the human mind. It follows that the supposed blindness of the French revolutionaries was only a necessary consequence of the natural functioning of the human mind. It was quite the opposite of anything contingent.

Moreover, when Tocqueville explains why the French Revolution proceeded in the manner of a religious revolution, he does not say that there was there anything accidental about this process, but restricts himself to the particular conditions of France in this epoch. The universal principles of the Revolution are the very ones of democracy. The principal elements of the doctrine of the French revolutionaries are the very ones that constitute "the philosophic method of Americans."[53] The same reasoning explains why the Revolution "could make itself understood by all and be capable of being imitated in a hundred different places at the same time"[54] and why democracy irresistibly pushes men and peoples to resemble each other.[55] The

Revolution could have been imitated everywhere because democracy leads individuals and peoples to resemble each other. And when Tocqueville notes that, for this reason, the Revolution had "itself become a kind of imperfect new religion,"[56] does he not invite us to see in democracy also a kind of new religion? Let us reread how he synthesizes these points when he talks of the generative principle of American democracy. In the United States, the dogma of sovereignty of the people is not an isolated doctrine unrelated either to habits or to the configuration of dominant ideas. On the contrary, it can be seen as the last link in a chain of opinions that envelops the whole Anglo-Saxon world. Providence has given to each individual, whoever he may be, the measure of reason necessary for him to rule himself in the things that interest him alone. "In the United States, this is the great maxim on which civil and political society rest. The father of the family applies it to his children, the master to his servants, the local community to those it administers, the counties to the local communities, the state to the counties, the Union to the states. Extending throughout the whole nation, it becomes the dogma of sovereignty of the people."[57] It is not by accident that the term "dogma" encapsulates this summary of the generative principle of American democracy.

Just as the dogmas of the Catholic Church rule over a religious society that was "foundation and model" of the political society of the *ancien régime*, so does the democratic dogma of sovereignty of the people rule over all aspects of the social and political life of the Americans and gives its distinct character to their religion. A society is always ultimately governed by a dogma, by "the last link in the chain of opinion" that binds the whole of society.

It is quite remarkable how the Americans, in the Tocquevillian description, conduct themselves with regard to their religion—broadly indifferent to dogmas, with little or no asceticism—and yet they call themselves Christians. In a certain sense, it is the outside observer, Tocqueville, who interprets this religious situation, thanks to the notion of natural religion. How might we define the religious nature of man? How do we

101

know what it is and how it expresses itself? Strictly speaking, one can know what the religious nature of man is and how it expresses itself only if God has revealed it. That is why Americans interpret the religious nature of man on the *basis* of revealed Christianity, which they apply to the secular state. There is no natural religion, only revealed religion reduced to the "natural" state by the necessities of democratic convention.

Thus, the idea of natural religion, which must limit and moderate democracy, is only one particular case of the democratic interpretation of man. According to this interpretation, because nature is strong by itself, because it is sufficient unto itself, no single human authority can claim to possess precise knowledge of it. No church can derive from a supposedly divine revelation the right to impose its dogmas, its organizational principles on the society that accepts its interpretation of the religious nature of man. Democratic convention gives itself the task of eroding authority, be it individual or institutional influences, so that nature alone makes its voice heard. We have seen that, pushed to its logical conclusion, such an interpretation endangers nature, in Tocqueville's view. Should we not also be afraid that, by the same mechanism, such an interpretation also endangers the religious nature of man?

This is what Tocqueville suggests, nowhere more clearly than in Chapter Seven, part one, volume II in *Democracy in America*, *"What Inclines the Spirit of Democratic Peoples Toward Pantheism."* This is what he writes of the condition of the human spirit in a democratic society: "The idea of uniformity obsesses the human spirit in democracies; it searches for uniformity everywhere and when the human spirit thinks it has found uniformity, it readily lays itself down in the bosom of uniformity and rests. Not only does it come to discover in the world one creation and one creator, this primordial division of things still bothers it, and it readily looks to expand and simplify its thought by including God and universe in a single whole. Among the different systems with whose aid philosophy looks to explain the universe, pantheism appears to be one of the best suited to seduce the human spirit in democratic countries. It is

102

against it that all those who stay enamored of the true grandeur of man must unite and fight."⁵⁸ It could not be said more clearly that the same process by which the democratic spirit "expands and simplifies" its ideas to deliver the diversity of the world to the power of uniformity (*semblable*)⁵⁹ also exercises itself at the expense of the only difference that natural religion maintains, that between creation and creator. It is the same spirit that causes historic individuals to disappear here below that abolishes the distinction between the here below and the beyond. This fundamental distinction on which Tocqueville grounds the possibility and the necessity of assuring religion a central place in democratic societies is but the ultimate victim of the democratic spirit. How can one make of this distinction the counterforce to oppose the perverse tendencies of this spirit that puts in danger "the true grandeur of man," since, as we have seen, the reduction of religion to this sole dimension—the idea of natural religion—is already the work of this democratic spirit?

The religion of Americans is certainly the precious moderator of their democracy. But it is the moderator of it only in being its artifice and, it is to be feared, its designated victim. By failing to establish the idea of natural religion as anything but a happy but provisional phase in the progress of the democratic spirit, Tocqueville can not find a point of anchorage in his thought that is independent of social convention, be it democratic or aristocratic. Religion itself, which in principle elevates men above all earthly things, can give itself to men only in a conventional setting, only in being authorized—in both senses of the term—by certain men and certain institutions.

Having said this, we can understand better Tocqueville's hesitations in his interpretation of the antireligious passions of the French revolutionaries, because we understand better what Tocqueville describes as their blindness. He presents them first attacking the Catholic religion because it found itself accidentally attached to a political order that the French revolution wanted to destroy. Afterwards, he shows them to us attacking this religion because of its very principles, which were "the foundation and model" of the political society of the *ancien régime*. The ambiguities—and finally, the untenable character—of its doctrine of natural religion established that this mixture of religion and politics is not accidental nor even peculiar to a particular society. This reciprocal dependence of the religious and the political is enshrined in the nature of things. One can only theoretically differentiate between the priest and the tithe-holder, for if the priest could cease to be a tithe-holder, he would then be, for example, a democratic citizen, with the advantages but also the constraints and limitations belonging to his new state. It is because he was tithe-holder that the priest of the *ancien régime* was a citizen of its society.

Tocqueville incontestably establishes this in the only passage in *The Old Regime* devoted to a somewhat detailed description of the clergy. This description is found, significantly, in Chapter Two of book II, "*Of the Kind of Freedom That Is Met With in the Ancien Regime And Its Influence on the Revolution.*" The principal characteristic of the Church at this time is its independence with regard to the central power. "The priests that one has often seen since, so servilely subjected in civil matters to no matter what temporal sovereign, and who are his most shameless flatterers for the sake of the slight favor the sovereign preferred the Church, then formed one of the most independent bodies in the nation and the only one whose particular freedoms commanded respect."[60] Tocqueville even adds that "at the heart of ecclesiastical power itself there were respected limits."[61] The principal reason for this was that the Church was a landowner. "But what contributed above all to giving priests the ideas, needs, sentiments, and often the passion of citizens was landed property."[62] Tocqueville indicates to us that, having read the court transcripts from ancient provincial states, he was able to realize to what extent the bishops and abbots, "among whom several were as eminent for their holiness as for their erudition,"[63] worried about the details of economic and social life and were competent in matters of agriculture and irrigation. Summarizing the results of his research, he concludes: "I don't know if, all things considered, and despite the stunning vices of several of its members, there was a clergy in the world more remarkable than the Catholic clergy of France at the moment when the Revolution took it by surprise—more enlightened, more nationally minded, less confined to the world of private matters alone, better endowed with public virtues, and at the same time, more full of faith. Their persecution well demonstrates what I say."[64] It was thus a kind of American clergy with faith, knowledge, and distinction to boot.

The religious order must therefore be part of the political order. The tithe-holding priest of the *ancien régime* was a citizen of his society in the same way as the American minister or priest is a citizen of his. It is because they are both citizens that the first guaranteed "the kind of freedom that was encountered in the *ancien régime*" and the second was the surest support of American democracy. The religious situation *after* the Revolution is the counterproof. In postrevolutionary France, the priest "is a stranger in the midst of civil society, in which almost none of its concerns can touch him directly. For his conscience, he depends only on the Pope; for his subsistence, only on the Prince. His only country is the Church. In each political event, he hardly sees anything but what can help or harm the Church. If the Church is free and prosperous, what does the rest matter? His most natural attitude in matters of politics is indifference. An excellent member of his Christian city, he is a mediocre citizen everywhere else. Such sentiments and related ideas in a body that is the preceptor of children and the guide for morals cannot fail to enervate the entire soul of the nation about what concerns public life."[65] In such a situation, religious society stands apart from political society but not independent of it, since it is the society or "the Prince" who furnishes it with material resources. The society or "the Prince" also furnishes them with a good part of their moral resources insofar as, after the revolutionary turmoil, a large part of society turns toward religion because of the idea they have of its social utility.[66] The landowners emerged from the Revolution in tears and became believers. Religion then conserved only enough force to weaken

105

civic spirit and thus to discredit itself in the eyes of the friends of political freedom. It was not possible for the priest to cease being a citizen. He became a bad one instead. We can appreciate Tocqueville when he sees in such a situation a state against nature. But in its "natural state," in America, religion, far from preserving for itself a real independence, gains its dividends only in fully recognizing its political dependence with regard to democracy.

This stated, it must be acknowledged that religion obtains its properly religious influence not in striving to assure its separation from the political order but in becoming a constituent part of the political order in which men are open to the influences that tear them from the narrow circle of their daily interests. We have seen that, in the eyes of Tocqueville, democratic man is the least so inclined, occupied as he is in having his ego inflated to the outer limits of the two worlds and then bringing these two worlds back to fit the dimensions and control of his petty self.

Religion occupies the strategic plane *par excellence* in the Tocquevillian doctrine. In it, he sees the practical possibility of effectively moderating democratic passions and the theoretical possibility of securing access, in the framework of a democratic society, to an outside, to a thing *other* than democracy, to pure nature, but by naturally religious man, free from all convention, even the convention of equality. He establishes this practical possibility only in abolishing its theoretical possibility. In analyzing his doctrine, we have come to realize that his pivot—the radical distinction between the religious and the political that is founded in nature—was either, at best, the protective and provisional myth of the democratic convention or, at worst, the reality of a society in which religion separates itself from the political order only to weaken the latter and to discredit itself. What Tocqueville calls the "natural state of men in matters of religion" recognizes in fact religion's total dependence on the democratic order, while its unnatural state is a state in which it continues to balk at this recognition, though at this point in time the principal support religion enjoys stems from the idea one has of its social utility.

Religion occupies the strategic plane *par excellence* also because it is in the difference between its unnatural and natural state that one sees exemplified the difference between democratic revolution and democracy, with France prey to democratic revolution and the United States peacefully enjoying a finished democracy. This difference is quite real, and Tocqueville demonstrates that in religious matters, the peaceful and prosperous American situation is the truth and—if men are prudent—the final outcome of the convulsive and unhealthy French situation. But at the same time, the war of opinion and the mixture of religion and politics that engenders this war speaks to a more fundamental truth. Religion can exist healthily and durably only by being part of the political order. One such order is democracy, which completely domesticates religion as and because it domesticates nature. The other is aristocracy, which leaves to religion an immensely powerful influence—to the point where religion becomes aristocracy's foundation and model—as it leaves a great influence to individual natures. The revolutionary mixing peculiar to France is only an illustration of the point so clearly highlighted but denied by Tocqueville. "Beside each religion is found a political opinion, which, through affinity, is joined to it. Let the human spirit follow its tendency, and it will regulate in a uniform manner, the political society and the divine city. It will seek, if I dare say so, to *harmonize* the earth and heaven."[67] It is this harmonization, naturally prone in certain circumstances to producing "mixings" of the two worlds that are in conformity with the nature of things. The rigorous distinction between the religious and the political, on the other hand, is only an instrument of the harmonization of religion with democratic politics. The revolutionary situation reveals a fundamental truth that democracy at peace obscures by fulfilling.

Chapter 9

DEMOCRACY AND DEMOCRATIC REVOLUTION

In the last chapter we used *The Old Regime and the French Revolution* to make Tocqueville's thought on the fundamental issue of religion clearer. We came to the conclusion that Tocqueville's thoughts on religion demonstrate no change in his fundamental principles, but that the necessity of making sense of very different phenomena caused these principles to be seen in another light. This helped us see more exactly the reasoning behind these principles, their scope, limits, and difficulties. Therein lies the principal interest in studying *The Old Regime and the French Revolution* for one who seeks to uncover the springs of Tocquevillian doctrine. Tocqueville's principles, which unfold abundantly and majestically in this work, are expressed in *Democracy* in tighter and more studied prose that frequently resorts to irony, even to sarcasm. The principles are always pregnant with meaning, but the writer often highlights them by giving them an epigrammatic form and scintillating expression. Certainly, American reality was in conformity with the principles while in this instance it is the contrary. But reading the *The Old Regime and the French Revolution*, we wonder if the bitterness that is poured into these pages stems only from the sadness of a good citizen who recapitulates the reasons for the long-term impotence of France to found free institutions. With each dig into the archives, he discovers that the French malady goes much further, or even, sometimes that the obdurate French reality goes so far as to put into question the validity of the principles themselves.

The general thesis of Tocqueville is simple and clear. The Revolution had neither as an object nor as an essential purpose to overturn religious beliefs and set social anarchy into play. Its object and its work were much more prosaic: to establish equality of conditions.[1] This work was in fact all the more limited because, in 1788, the *ancien régime* was already more than half destroyed. The leitmotif of Chapter Five of Book I deals with *"The Proper Work of the French Revolution."* It can truly be said that the entire work finds quintessential expression in the following phrase: The Revolution is only. . . "This Revolution had had for its sole effect the abolition of those political institutions . . . ordinarily deemed 'feudal' and their replacement with a more uniform and simple social and political order that had equality of conditions as its basis."[2] "It was only the completion of a long travail, the sudden and violent termination of a work in which ten generations of men had toiled. The Revolution brought to an end suddenly, by a convulsive and painful effort, without transition, caution, or respect, what could have been accomplished by itself little by little in the long run. Such was the work of the Revolution."[3] "The *ancien régime* lent to the Revolution several of its forms. What the latter did was only to add the atrocity of its genius to it."[4] This reduction of the Revolution to what would be accomplished over centuries by the old regime belies the Revolution's significance. "It appeared to be even greater than it was."[5] In other words, it simply made visible what already was there. At the end of an article Tocqueville wrote in 1836, a sketch of the *ancien régime*,[6] one finds a striking formulation of this point. "All that the Revolution did was being done, I have no doubt, without it. It was only a violent and rapid process that was furthered by the adaption of the political state to the social state, facts to ideas, and laws to mores."[7]

The whole task of Tocqueville will be to show how, during the centuries that preceded the Revolution, the social state, ideas, and mores had become more and more democratic, a radical transformation to which the Revolution had nothing to add but its bloody significance. The instrument of this transformation from feudal society to democratic society was the monarchy. The term "instrument" is appropriate because, in the old regime, the fundamental division remains the dichotomy between aristocracy and democracy. The monarchy had no particular identity of its own. What caused it to be what it was depended on its social predicate. It was feudal-aristocratic, then absolutist-democratic. More precisely, the absolute monarchy had no proper identity of its own because it profited from the social interregnum between aristocracy and the coming of the people.[8] The aristocracy/democracy dichotomy is the determinative categorization because the social state is the generative fact. "The real object of the Revolution had been much less a form of government than a social form, less the conquest of political rights than the destruction of privileges."[9]

Tocqueville gives a political interpretation of the passage from one social state to another. How, in effect, did royal power bring about the democratization of society? It did so essentially by a methodical erosion of the political power of the nobility. Feudal society is an aristocratic society. The nobility is its governing body. "In feudal times, the nobility were looked on in the same manner as one looks on the government today."[10]

This political dispossession of the nobility explains most of the characteristics of the *ancien régime* that led to the Revolution and in particular the condition of the peasants with its attendant paradoxes. In the eighteenth century, the peasant had only just ceased being a serf and become a landholder.[11] At the same time, he had withdrawn from the government of his lords.[12] Thus, with "feudal rights" having entirely ceased to exist, a tax imposed by the nobility in compensation for its government appeared irksome even if in itself the tax did not represent much money. The peculiar situation of the nobles evolved out of this. "The lord is in reality but a man with privileges and immunities that separate him from all others. His situation is different, not his power. *The lord is only the first in-*

111

habitant, intendants were careful to point out in their letters to their subdelegates."[13] Even if the nobles stayed on the land because their finances did not let them reside in Paris, they could hardly have a feeling of responsibility with regard to the peasants they no longer governed. "These men were no longer his subjects: he was no longer a fellow citizen. This was unique in history and led to a sort of absenteeism of the heart."[14]

What was true of the nobles is true of all rich landowners, who hastened to turn themselves into bourgeoisie in the cities—transferring their tax exemptions there—as soon as their finances permitted. "In these circumstances, the peasant appears almost entirely separated from the upper classes."[15] Thus, peasants were more abandoned than oppressed by the upper classes who, for their part, constantly enriched themselves. Such powerlessness made it convenient to call on them when it was a matter of raising state revenues with the result that, "despite the progress of civilization, the condition of the French peasant was sometimes worse in the eighteenth century than it had been in the thirteenth."[16] In a word, "civilization turned against itself."[17]

If circumstances no longer allowed the nobles to rule the peasants, with even greater force they no longer allowed them to rule the bourgeoisie. Or rather, the nobles no longer governed with the bourgeoisie. Both classes had been dispossessed by the royal power of the part of the government they enjoyed up until the sixteenth century.

> In effect, as the government of the lords fell apart, as the convening of the Estates General became rare or ceased, and as the general freedoms ended up succumbing and led local freedoms to their ruin, the bourgeois and the gentleman no longer had any contact in public life. They no longer even felt the need to meet one another and make themselves understood. They daily grew more independent of one another. And they also became strangers to one another. By the eighteenth century, this revolution was complete. These two men no longer met except by chance in their private lives. The two classes no longer felt themselves merely rivals, they became enemies.[18]

Thus, the Third Estate got rich, cultivated themselves and in the end rose to the level of the nobility, which they even passed sometimes. The nobility grew poorer, at least relatively. Equally rendered docile by the royal power, the individuals of these two classes could only devote themselves to their private possessions. Consequently, the members of these classes resembled each other more and more. But the historical legacy of inequality of conditions held them separate, and the absence of political freedom and a shared public space allowed them to live in complete ignorance of each other. The reverse situation prevailed in feudal times. "If you study how things happened in the first Estates General, you see a completely different scene. The bourgeois and the noble then had interests and affairs more in common. Much less mutual animosity was in evidence, though they still seemed to belong to two distinct races."[19] We are confronted here, on a much grander scale, with what Tocqueville observed in the laboratory of equality, to wit, the master/servant relationship in democratic society, which, in democratic society, manifests a paradoxical affinity between inequality and familiarity on the one hand, and equality and separation on the other.[20] But the change in scale opens the way to a crucial insight. It is political freedom that preserves the bond between markedly different and unequal social groups. It is political freedom that guarantees a strong union of aristocrat and commoner without in the slightest way reducing their inequality. This is because the social classes to which they belong must relate to each other in a public life where they are both participants. Tocqueville finds another example of this phenomenon in eighteenth century England, "where the different classes, although solidly attached to one another by common interests, still often differed in spirit and mores. Political freedom, which possesses the admirable power to foster relationships between citizens and mutual links of dependence, did not for that make them similar in every particular. In the long term, however, only the rule of a single person always and inevitably makes men grow similar to each other and mutually indifferent to their fates."[21]

If we compare the respective situations of the nobles and the Third Estate, in the feudal-aristocratic monarchy and in the democratic-monarchy, we see the following. In the former, an enormous difference exists in social conditions, power, riches, and mores, and in the mutual relations that occur within political institutions, conflict, collaboration, and familiarity between the classes. In the latter, differences in riches, mores, and power hardly exist any longer, but relations are rare, haphazard, and uniquely confined to private life, which contributes to the separation of the two classes and their mutual hostility. What explains this change is the transformation of the relation of each individual to his class and to the body politic as a whole. The disappearance of political freedom, the submission of all to the Prince, is one with the emancipation of the bourgeois and the noble in relation to their respective classes. "As a man, the bourgeois of the fourteenth century is undoubtedly greatly inferior to the bourgeois of the eighteenth century. But the bourgeoisie then as a body occupied a much more assured and elevated rank in political society."[22] As far as the nobility: "at the same time that the aristocratic order lost in this way their political power, gentlemen individually acquired several privileges that they had never possessed or aggrandized those that they already had. It could be said that the members enriched themselves from the spoils of their corporate existence."[23] Unequal social conditions are no longer the basis on which the political body functions; rather, they now define for their individual members the possibilities—unequal—of appropriating goods of all sorts available in society. To belong to the nobility no longer means participating in the government. It is to have reserved access to the best places and the choicest morsels. But this monopoly of access is difficult to maintain when one no longer holds political power. It is necessary to rely on the Prince to guarantee the privileges of the nobility. No matter how well disposed he is, nothing guarantees that his idea of his interest will coincide with the nobility's. Above all, to think that the Prince will support and favor the nobility because he is well disposed to them is a very weak supposition, given that the mate-

114

rial and immaterial goods produced in and by society increasingly escape the control and influence of the nobility once it is
deprived of political power and therefore of a great part of its
social and moral influence. What this society produces in
wealth or ideas is produced without the decisive participation
of the nobility but with the decisive participation of the Third
Estate and to a greater extent by the upper stratum of this class.
The intervention of the Prince, the persistence of traditions, can
at best preserve for the nobility only a weak and diminishing
part of the goods produced in its absence. All the rest go to the
upper stratum of the Third Estate. The decreasing fraction that
is still apportioned to the nobility can only engender increasing
revulsion to its parasitism on the part of society. In the last
decades of the *ancien régime*, as civilization turned against the
peasant, it likewise turned against the nobility, albeit in a very
different fashion. The nobility still took the best part for itself,
as it constituted the ornament of society. But the progress of
civilization takes place more and more outside it and therefore
against it. The nobility is more and more superfluous. It was
told so and it repeated the same thing with insistence. And it
was made to see itself so.

The end of the *ancien régime* witnessed the irritated vanity
of the Third Estate along with that of nobiliary pride. The
background of social homogeneity that gave rise to this double
irritation was indicative of both a resistance to and an avowal
of an already present social equality. "Each of them [the Third
Estate and the nobility] held to its particular station because
others defined themselves by it. But they were all ready to mix
in the same mass provided no one had anything apart and did
not rise above the common level."[24] Once the social classes
were in a certain sense privatized by the concentration of all
political power in the hands of the Prince, the position of each
social class was appropriated by the individuals who comprised
it, who were privatized and individualized in turn. The social
ranks ceased to be the points of orientation for the public space
the moment they entered into the sphere of individual private
possession.

At this moment, class struggle occurs in its proper sense. The appropriation or privatization of a social class by the individuals who comprise it closes that class in upon itself, and it in fact becomes a social world apart from others and can entertain the illusion of its own self-sufficiency. In such a situation, the other class has no right to exist. It should moreover be noted that in the case of the Third Estate, this illusion had a certain justification. The way Sieyès formulated it, with an incisiveness that history would not forget, was that the Third Estate was more than an order or a class but was rather a complete nation, that had no need of the nobles in order to exist and that could get along much better once these latter were sent back to the forests of Franconia. What this vision ignores, however, is that the Third Estate could effectively do without the privileged because the freedom that formerly was vested in the latter had been taken over by the central power.

Tocqueville makes classes and their struggle the spring of the French Revolution, in the first volume of the *The Old Regime and the French Revolution* that he finished and published,[25] as well as in the sketches of the second that were to be devoted to the history of revolutionary events, as such.[26] But what he always insists on is that the class struggle in the precise sense— that is to say, a struggle that aims at the destruction or at least the complete subjugation of the opposing class—only unfolds in a particular situation, precisely in that society where the classes in struggle have been deprived of political freedom by the absolute power.[27]

Tocqueville's analysis ultimately hinges on things political. What he describes, in analyzing the equalization of conditions in the *ancien régime*, is what takes place in a society when political freedom has disappeared. What he describes is the effect of an absence. The logic of the social process forces us to see the equalization of conditions, the homogenization and separation of individuals, as taking place in the vacuum of political freedom, which is the cause of the particular form that the process takes.

The abolition of political freedom does not mean the abolition of all liberty in the *ancien régime* as Chapter Two of Book II, "*Of the Kind of Freedom Which Is Met in the Ancien Regime and of Its Influence on the Revolution,*" attests. The freedom that survived in the *ancien régime* was derived from the survival of aristocratic elements, whether as traditions of pride in the aristocracy properly understood or whether under those of privileges—guaranteed by property—of the clergy. Thanks to these aristocratic elements, social separation had not yet attained its final limit. "No one was able to lose himself in the crowd and go hide his servile behavior. Each man found himself there as if in a very small theater, it is true, but one very well lit, and there was always the same public to applaud or boo."[28] But this irregular and bizarre freedom essentially had its place outside of the political spectrum in civil society.

> Be attentive to the fact that political society was without common bonds, but that civil society still had some. One was bound to another within the classes. There even remained something of the tight bond that had existed between the noble class and the people. Although this happened in civil society, the consequences made themselves felt indirectly in political society. Men thus linked formed irregular and unorganized masses that were, however, resistant to the hand that held power. The Revolution, having broken these social bonds without establishing political bonds in their place, had prepared equality and servitude at the same time.[29]

The more the effects of the disappearance of political freedom made itself felt, the more social equality prevailed, the more political freedom would become necessary.

From where does this freedom, so necessary and often so absent, come? "I often wondered what was the source of this passion for political freedom that in all times has caused men to do the greatest things. In what sentiments is it rooted and nourished?"[30] The response is disappointing and firm.

> What in all times has attached the heart of certain men so strongly to it are its attractions, its unique charm, independent of

117

its benefits. It is the pleasure to speak, act, breathe without constraint under the sole government of God and laws. He who looks to freedom for something other than itself is made to serve. Do not ask me to analyze this sublime taste. It must be experienced. It enters of itself into the great hearts that God has prepared to receive it. It fills and inflames them. One can give up trying to make mediocre souls who have never felt it understand it.[31]

This political freedom, whose presence or absence is so important for the general destiny of societies, thus has its source in an unanalyzable and incommunicable experience, as a gift given directly by nature or God to certain men. In such a way, the alternative between the two forms of freedom—as aristocratic privilege and as shared rights in democracy—are only seemingly overcome. On the one hand, political freedom is the most indispensable thing for men if they want to lead a fully human life, since "it creates the light that allows us to see and judge the vices and virtues of men."[32] On the other hand, the presence of this essential component of human life is not guaranteed. (One does not find the love of freedom in all men. Far from it.) Nor is it susceptible to being produced at will by men. (Its only source is in nature.) This sovereign, illusive thing gives rise to equality and inequality and, to a certain degree, reconciles them. Between unequals, it causes familiarity, collaboration, mutual bonds, and a certain degree, at least, of mutual recognition to penetrate society. As for equals, inclined to withdraw into themselves, political freedom causes them to venture outside themselves to work in the public space on common projects. Thanks to political freedom, the unequal forgets his conventional superiority or inferiority. The equal makes use of his restricted sovereignty. Both enter into a *humanum commune* where the interchange of public words and actions puts individuals in contact, nature against nature, with their own virtues and vices, without their conventional inequality or equality to veil from their eyes or the eyes of others what they value and what they are capable of. The fact remains that the source of this political life is in a gift that nature dispenses unequally.

118

This gift of nature is fertile only because it is unequal. In effect, if the love of freedom were equally inscribed in each man, it would be a necessary and universal component of social life. Men could therefore count on it and use it in their plans and calculations as they could count on the taste for material goods. Freedom would be at their mercy, nature at the mercy of their convention. Freedom would not "create the light that allows us to see and judge the vices and virtues of men" if it were a requisite component of the eye of each individual.

This conception of political freedom stands outside of the aristocratic and democratic dichotomy because it is founded on a different interpretation of human freedom. Aristocratic freedom is founded on the particular right—the privilege—of certain men; democratic freedom on the universal and equal rights of all men. In the usual Tocquevillian presentation, such as the 1836 article, that gives the most precise formulation, the two forms of freedom are different only in extent. That is why the one whose extension coincides with humanity itself is alone just. The restrictedness and artificiality of aristocratic convention give men great virtues for bad reasons. Aristocratic convention denatures them in a fortunate way. The justice and justness of democratic convention relaxes in them the bonds of civic virtues. Democrats generalize their civic virtues to such a point that they tend to confuse them with simple universal moral virtues.[33] The aristocratic civic sense is too narrow to be just. The democratic civic sense is too extensive to be strong. Aristocratic freedom affirms the unequal; democratic freedom affirms the equal. Both affirm a relation between men. When Tocqueville presents the source of political freedom as an individual "taste," as a "gift" of nature, he totally changes the register of his voice. He has rooted it in something that is not a relation between men but a quality, a virtue of certain individuals. Or, it is a relation of the individual to himself. This last definition lies outside the dichotomy of the two social definitions, as nature lies outside of convention, although freedom thus defined inspires the best of what man can realize under the two conditions.

119

In the chapter concluding *The Old Regime and the French Revolution*, entitled *"How the Revolution Emerged by Itself From What Preceded It,"* Tocqueville writes the following: "In reading this book, those who have attentively studied the France of the eighteenth century have been able to see grow and develop in its breast two main passions, which were not contemporaneous and did not always tend toward the same goal. The one, more profound and longer in developing, was violent and inextinguishable hatred of inequality. This was born and was nourished by the sight of this very inequality. . . . The other, more recent and less rooted, inclined men to wish to live not only as equals, but free."[34] The unequal force of the two passions explains why the Revolution established equality of conditions without succeeding in establishing political freedom. This asymmetry, which Tocqueville here links to the peculiarities of French history, he makes in *Democracy in America* a general characteristic of democracy as such. "Political freedom from time to time gives a certain number of citizens sublime pleasures. Equality furnishes each day small pleasures to each man. . . . The passion that equality engenders must be simultaneously energetic and general."[35] What the history of France brilliantly shows, American democracy also gives witness to, although in a more veiled fashion. In this sense, the Revolution is the revelation of democracy.

The discouraging absence of political freedom in French history (unlike in America history, where it is constantly visible) forces the question of the ultimate origin of the matrix of political freedom that Tocqueville finds in an unanalyzable passion of certain men. This absence also forces us rigorously to differentiate between independence and freedom. Tocqueville compares French citizens in privileged classes before the Revolution to their English contemporaries.

> It could be said that a Frenchman belonging to these classes in the eighteenth century often found it much easier to resist the government and to force it to act with moderation than an Englishman would have found it at the same time and in the same

situation. In certain instances, power believed itself under the obligation to defer and to proceed more temperately and with a more circumspect step than the English government felt itself to be with regard to a citizen of the same category. So far is one wrong in confusing independence with freedom. No one is less independent than a free citizen.[36]

The idea of freedom that inspires the Americans, the dogma of sovereignty of the people, is essentially expressed in terms of individual independence. Certainly Tocqueville describes at length the institutions that allow Americans to overcome this independence, this separation. But never does he indicate in what virtue and what passion these institutions have their source. Although he methodically traces their Puritan geneal-ogy, he never tells us that they have their origin in the same pas-sion that occasions an outpouring of such emotion in the *an-cien régime*. What is more, he links the moral life of Americans in this matter to a rejection of any too-exalted notion of virtue. He links it to the doctrine of self-interest rightly understood.

Tocqueville attributes sufficient importance to this point to devote two chapters to it.[37] Americans "do their utmost to prove that the interest of each is to be honest" and "willingly to sacrifice to the good of the state a part of their time and wealth."[38] Tocqueville does not disclose whether the reasons advanced by American moralists for this doctrine have con-vinced him or not. "Suffice it to say that they have convinced their fellow citizens."[39] But if he does not judge the ultimate value of this doctrine, he is very certain of its advantages.

Self-interest rightly understood is not a very lofty doctrine, but it is clear and sure. It does not seek to attain grand objects, but it attains those that it aims at without too much effort. Since it is in the reach of all levels of intelligence, each individual easily grasps and holds it without difficulty. In adapting itself in mar-velous fashion to the weaknesses of men, it easily obtains great empire over men. It is not difficult to maintain it, as it turns per-sonal interest against itself and, to govern the passions, makes use of the stimulant that excites them. I am not afraid to say that

121

the doctrine of self-interest rightly understood seems to me, of all philosophic theories, most appropriate to the needs of our time, and I see in it the most powerful protection against themselves that remains for them. Therefore, it is principally toward the doctrine of self-interest rightly understood that the moralists of our day must turn. Even though they judge it imperfect, it would still be imperative to adopt it as necessary.[40]

It is important to quote Tocqueville at length on this point. To do so just after quoting him on the subject of love of political freedom is enough to make clear that the spring of free institutions of Americans is not the love of political freedom, such as moves Tocqueville. Passing from the latter to the former we traverse a moral universe. Certainly, Tocqueville does not exclude the possibility that certain Americans can sometimes be moved by pure love of freedom and virtue, even when they invoke the doctrine of self-interest rightly understood.[41] But their habits are founded on this latter principle, the doctrine of self-interest rightly understood. Only it is adapted to the needs of democratic society, since it alone is "in the reach of all intellects."

From this perspective, the difference between France and the United States narrows. "On the whole, I do not think that there is more egoism among us than in America. The only difference is that there it is enlightened and here it is not."[42] Of freedom, there is not a word.

In the *ancien régime*, the democratization of society lets loose all its tendencies to separate men and unfolds society's natural defects. This is so precisely because the political order is occupied and protected by an institution—royalty—that has a non-democratic origin and that, even where it has ceased to be feudal and has become the instrument of democracy, obeys a principle other than democracy.[43] Monarchy is an instrument of democracy, but it is a perverse instrument because it grants democracy dispensation from governing *itself*. The bad effects of the separation of men are unmitigated. Emigration did for the English who became Americans what royalty did for the French. It withdrew them from feudal influences. The sea did the work of the king, and landed space did the work of centuries. The American democracy, having placed an entire ocean between it and the Old World, was forced to govern itself with no resources other than its own. Simply to survive, it had to invent procedures that overcame the natural separateness that existed among equal individuals. Because the American democracy is pure democracy, it is moderate and free democracy. But to say that it is pure democracy means only that democracy in America had to confront political necessity alone, alone had to take charge of politics.

At the same time, Providence had freed American democracy from two terrible necessities that weighed upon previous political organizations: the scarcity of natural resources and the presence of powerful foreign enemies. That is why political freedom in the full sense of the term, that which unites citizens in public, was subject to the test of the harshest necessity and therefore could manifest itself as an outgrowth of independence, natural to democracy and not sundered from it. The doctrine of self-interest rightly understood is suitable for men where no deadly peril, domestic or foreign, threatens it.[44] It could not inspire the Gettysburg Address.

The two great versions of democracy in whose comparison Tocqueville grounds its nature are two great experiments, thanks to which one can observe the radically new problems that the existence and progress of democracy pose in all its aspects, particularly politics. The idea of democracy and the idea of politics are two entirely different notions, extrinsic to one another. The notion of modern democracy is not political. Democracy is an all-inclusive opinion that speaks to the totality of human things. It has disruptive consequences in the political order because it attacks what had been the presupposition of all political existence, whatever the regime, namely the bonds of dependence, individual influences, the hierarchy of notables and their solicitude for others—the stuff of political life from time immemorial. By lodging independence and separation there, where no previous regime—no matter how democratic it was— had thought to lodge it, it disrupted the very material out of which the political order is constructed, what Tocqueville calls the "social state."

Under the sway of such an opinion, political freedom is nothing but a particular case of the application of the principle of human independence. It is the application of a principle that must prevail in all branches of human life and becomes, by this very fact, a particular branch of human life. Democratic freedom, that is to say, individual independence, becomes political freedom only because men can not escape the necessity of living together. Left to themselves, freed of this necessity, it would produce only a "dis-society", a dispersion, like what reigned in the American West.[45] Thus, when men fallen prey to the democratic idea are held together by a preexisting State of another origin, as in France, they accommodate themselves very well to this situation, for the idea they have formed of their condition is apolitical, and to that extent antipolitical. The perverse compatibility between the democratic state and political despotism stems from the fact that democracy and despotism are apolitical and, to that extent, anti-political. (The despot concentrates in a sole person the whole political life of the society over which he reigns.) But this agreement does not suppose a necessary link because, by another natural compatibility, this time fortunate, democratic men, who wish to be independent, wish to be so also in the political sphere.[46]

If democratic men are citizens, they can be only free citizens. But they are not willingly citizens because civic life presupposes the abandonment of this individual independence that has totally gained their favor. Consequently, they are not willingly free citizens. The democratic dogma thus engenders indifference to public things. And since civic life presupposes the abandonment of the independence to which democratic men are devoted, it pushes men along the line of least resistance to accede to despotism, provided that it preserves the appearance of independence, that is to say, invokes the democratic dogma.[47]

Political freedom, which is the subject of the most beautiful exaltations in the *The Old Regime and the French Revolution*, has no commensurate force in the dogma of sovereignty of the people. This dogma makes room for individual independence only by analogy, a reflection of political freedom that is presented as an adaptation, grounded on the doctrine of self-interest rightly understood. The absence of this analogue or reflection in French history makes us understand the relation between democracy and political freedom better than does its presence in the American Republic. The pathos of the *ancien régime* leads us on the path to a truth more bitter but more complete than that put forward by the abundant, easy, and often happy prose of *Democracy*.

In this way alone can we understand the ardent admiration of Tocqueville for "our fathers of 1789" and the Constituent Assembly.[48] This admiration goes against the *whole* Tocquevillian analysis of the meaning of the Revolution, as Gobineau told him in acid but accurate terms.[49] The grandeur of 1789 for Tocqueville lies not in its results. It is in the event itself, in its own glow, and is self-contained. It is a great act of political freedom, even if it did not succeed in establishing political freedom for even the shortest period of time, even if it made servitude worse. The democratic principle of individual independence does not allow us to understand the grandeur of 1789, does not comprehend it, because it obscures the specifically holy character of the political order in making of this order a particular case for the application of its dogma.

Democracy is a dogma. This dogma postulates that independence is the natural state of man, that the humanity of man is entirely contained in each individual. The humanity of man is, in right, if not in fact, separable from the body politic in which he lives. What tradition thought was the result of a rigorous exercise of civic and moral virtues—with the aid of Fortune or the grace of God—namely, to live free, democracy holds as the minimal requisite of humanity. Independence must therefore find a place in all human relations—between men and women, father and children, master and servant, between man and God. All branches of human life must be organized in conformity with this dogma. Democracy lays down as a necessary beginning what tradition judged the ultimate and fragile achieve-

125

ment. The whole economy of human life finds itself radically modified by it.

It is necessary to break down then recompose human life according to this formula. All the moral contents of this life have been fixed in predemocratic epochs, and the democratic dogma has no moral content, or this moral content resides entirely in the affirmation of individual independence or autonomy. The individual can legitimately obey only a law that he has given himself. But what law will an individual without law give himself? The democratic dogma is purely formal, dizzyingly empty. The life of democratic men will therefore be made up of compromises between the contents of inherited morality and the democratic formula. It is one of those compromises, fortunately, that Tocqueville finds in the American way of life. The palladium of Americans is their religion.

The exquisite Tocquevillian tension lies here. He adheres to the democratic formula and judges it just. He perceives with an unequaled acuity its dizzyingly destructive effects. Just as the American citizen recurs to a modified Christianity to protect himself from the dizziness of his unlimited freedom, so Tocqueville overcomes this tension by an appeal to Providence. He can not help but see that the progress of democracy puts in peril human greatness. "It is natural to believe that what most satisfies the gaze of the Creator and Protector of men is not the exceptional prosperity of a few but the greatest well-being of all. What seems to me a decline is therefore in his eyes a progress; what offends me is agreeable to Him. Equality is less elevated, perhaps, but it is more just and its justice is the stuff of its grandeur and beauty. I strive to share this perspective of God, and it is from its vantage that I seek to consider and judge human things."[50] But Tocqueville is not satisfied with this sacrifice of his intellect, and if he believes that God approves of what he deplores, he knows what human freedom is. He does not discard what he feels in his soul so that it is pleasing to the supposed judgment of God. His entire task is to indicate ways to preserve freedom under democratic dogma.

Does Tocqueville believe in this God, friend and author of

democracy? No one knows. But it is by His intercession alone that he feels the strength to consent to democracy. Religious faith alone allows him to confront "religious terror" in the face of democracy.

This terrifying democracy is not divine; the God who allows one to look at it without blinking is undoubtedly not divine either. But it is by this compromise with the idea of God that Tocqueville finds the strength to will and find hope in political freedom, as it is in the compromise with Christianity that Americans find the means to maintain and make prosper political freedom under democratic dogma.

CONCLUSION

It is difficult to be a friend of democracy, but it is necessary to be a friend of democracy. Such is the teaching of Tocqueville. It is difficult to be a friend of democracy because the democratic dogma is destructive of the moral contents that constitute the uniqueness of humanity and therefore its grandeur. It is necessary to be a friend of democracy because in this condition alone is it possible to preserve under the democratic dogma, at least by reflection or analogy, and often or sometimes in accord with the virtue of men, the reality of these moral contents. In particular, only by fully accepting the democratic principle is it possible to maintain or give rise to political freedom. In the exercise of political freedom, men have access to a *humanum commune* where they forget convention and overcome the dizziness of absolute individual independence, the foundation of the democratic dogma. It is true that democracy is in a very real sense the enemy of human grandeur, but the enemies of democracy are much more dangerous enemies of this grandeur.

Democracy has two sets of enemies. The first refuse the principle of democracy, the equality of men, which they judge contrary to natural inequality. They wish to stop the progress of equality and restore the supposedly natural and necessary inequalities. They do not know what they are doing or what they want. First, they misconstrue the force of democracy in that it already has changed all relations. Next, they suppose that they know what the nature of man is and how political society is to be constructed to conform to this nature. They believe that the nature of man is easy to know and that it only asks to be affirmed. Thus, they fully share the democratic prejudice. They are able only to destroy the good of which democracy is capable and to add to its faults. They can only proliferate the faults peculiar to inequality by using the faults peculiar to equality. Also, because defeated in advance, they only leave ruins, on which the equality that they blindly hate will establish a more restrictive empire than the one they have tried to abolish. In the eyes of civilized men, they will have compromised the moral contents that democracy effectively threatens and that must be preserved.

Democracy must also confront a second category of enemy, which one could call its excessive or immoderate friends. They claim only to be reasonable democrats, and since democracy is based on equality, they want to realize this equality. Equality is only formal; they wish to make it real. First, they misconstrue to what extent the formal character of democracy produces real effects. It is because democratic equality is "only" formal that it tends to establish itself in all human relations. To want to realize equality concretely means necessarily to limit its field of application to the target in the present by political action with that aim. This action seems to require a willingness to establish new inequalities. Above all, the claim to move beyond formal equality to its realization means refusing to admit the principle of formal equality, not only where democracy wishes to establish it but exactly where aristocratic societies judged it fitting and just. It is therefore to set up a type of inequality that the most inegalitarian societies of the past had never imagined and that would have horrified them. But this claim is also and at the same time to bring to their culmination the faults of democracy. The democratic convention, in itself, strictly abstract and therefore, in a sense, strictly inhuman, is continually humanized, in democratic societies, by the compromises that it must make with the necessities of social life, the moral contents inherited from predemocratic epochs, and finally with the irrepressible spontaneity of human nature. These immoderate friends of democracy refuse these compromises under the pretext that these compromises will maintain and even engender inequalities contrary to democratic principle. At this point, they strive to subject all aspects of human life, not to a dogma or doctrine, as one so inappropriately accuses them and as a point of pride they boast about so complacently, but to a pure Negation. This is because to want to realize the democratic abstraction, which contains nothing human, is to want to realize the unrealizable, and the effort to realize the unrealizable can only be considered the destruction of all that is really human.

The immoderate friends of democracy are incomparably more numerous than its enemies. In formal agreement with the principle of democracy, they easily flatter the passions of democratic men, claiming to fulfill the great democratic work that, without them, would remain suspended. They gain the respect of many in the confusion and tumult of democratic politics. They alone display constancy in the pursuit of a single goal. Those whose passions are not flattered and who do not show respect, they intimidate. This is because their actions, so strange and at times so violent, are always rigorously reduced to the democratic principle. To oppose them completely and to designate them as enemies of democracy, is to be understood as having renounced the principle of democracy itself. But here is the most abundant source of their strength. Democratic men, objects more than authors of the miserable movement toward the equalization of conditions, obscurely feel, as Tocqueville says, that the progress of equality is the "past, present, and future" of their history. The advantages and inconveniences of equality are matters to discuss. But what is beyond discussion is that this progress of equality is irresistible. These immoderate friends of equality have the pretension to set themselves up as the interpreters and conscious authors of this necessary historic process. They say they will what other men are subjected to. They call obeying necessity freedom. Their pretension satisfies both the laziness and the pride native to democratic man. Every man who participates in this enterprise identifies himself through the very fact of historical necessity. They take part in the omnipotence of History. This History, because it is strictly necessary, is no longer made by living men. Because he identifies himself with the cause itself of human things, the participant in this enterprise in the end completely escapes the necessity of recognizing the existence of other men and the objectivity of the world. He is the self-contained Whole. He achieves the "pantheist" dream of democratic man, who swallows the world in a yawn. He alone believes himself conscious and awake among an ignorant and sleepwalking humanity. In truth, he stupefies this democratic humanity that seeks, with more or less success, to stay awake. His dizzying assurances he gives as to a sleepwalker with whom, in each association, in each institution, in each man, he walks. He maintains equilibrium by crushing all that is free, all that is happy, all that has a human shape.

To love democracy well, it is necessary to love it moderately.

NOTES

PREFACE

1. This disquisition appears in Jean-Claude Lamberti. *Tocqueville and the Two Democracies* (Cambridge: Harvard University Press. 1989).

INTRODUCTION

1. Alexis de Tocqueville. *De la Démocratie en Amerique.* vol. 1. Oeuvres complètes de A. Tocqueville. tome premier (Paris: Gallimard. 1951). 14 (20). All references are to this edition and to its companion volume. *De la Démocratie en Amerique.* vol. II. (Paris: Gallimard.1951). [Translator's note: all translations from Tocqueville are our own. A reference to the equivalent page in the standard George Lawrence translation of *Democracy in America* edited by J. P. Mayer (New York: Doubleday. 1969) is contained parenthetically after the reference to the Gallimard edition of *Democracy in America.* For example. in this note (20) refers to the page number in the Lawrence–Mayer edition that corresponds to the reference from the Gallimard edition cited by Manent.]
2. Ibid.. 14 (20).
3. Ibid.. 4 (12).
4. Ibid.
5. Ibid.. 5 (12).
6. Ibid.. 2 (10).

7. Ibid., 11 (18).

8. Ibid., 12 (19).

9. Ch. 1: *The Geographic Configuration of North America.*

10. Ibid., 21, 25 (26, 30).

11. Ibid., 25 (30); Tocqueville's emphasis.

12. Ch. 2: *Concerning the Point of Departure of the Anglo-Americans and Its Importance to Their Future.*

13. Ibid., 31 (36). Tocqueville's emphasis.

14. Ibid., 34 (39).

15. See "Introduction": "The emigrants who settled in America at the beginning of the 17th century disengaged the principle of democracy from all those which it struggled against among the old societies of Europe and they transplanted it alone on the shores of the New World." 11 (18).

16. "However, nothing coarse could be detected in them. On the contrary, there prevailed in their manner of acting an habitual reserve and a kind of aristocratic politeness." 23 (28).

17. Ibid., 25 (30).

18. Ibid., 28 (32); See also: "I seem to see the whole destiny of America contained in the first Puritan." 292 (279).

19. Ibid., 1 (9).

20. Ibid., 11 (18).

21. Ibid.

CHAPTER ONE

1. Alexis de Tocqueville, *De la Démocratie en Amerique*, vol. 1, Oeuvres complètes de A. Tocqueville, tome premier (Paris: Gallimard, 1951), 1 (9). All references are to this edition and to its companion volume, *De la Démocratie en Amerique*, vol. II, (Paris: Gallimard, 1951).

2. Ibid., I: 11 (18).

3. See I: 331 (316): "Such themes that bear on my subject are not under consideration here; they are American without being democratic. . . ."

4. Ibid., I: 52 (56–57).

5. Ibid., I: 53 (57): "Two great political consequences affecting peoples are derived from the same social state: the consequences differ prodigiously from one to the other, but both are derived from the same fact."

6. Ibid., I: 45 (50). A little later in the same chapter (*"The Social State of the Anglo-Americans"*) of the "social state of different peoples whose political laws are merely an expression thereof," 47 (51).

7. Ibid., I: 53 (57).

8. Ibid., I: 54 (58).

9. Ibid., I: 54–55 (58).

10. Ibid., I: 55 (59).

11. Ibid., I: 56 (60).

12. Ibid., I: 55 (59).

13. Ibid., I: 46–47 (51–52).

14. Ibid., I: 36 (41).

15. Ibid., I: 57 (61).

16. See also I: 244 (233–34)

17. Ibid., I: 56 (60).

18. Ibid., I: 69 (72).

19. Ibid., I: 72 (74).

20. Ibid., I: 88 (89).

21. Ibid., I: 126 (124–25).

22. Ibid., I: 126 (125).

23. Ibid., I: part one, ch. 3 *in princ.*

24. Ibid., I: 63 (63).

25. Ibid., I: 56 (60). "The people reign in the American political world as God does in the universe. It is the cause and the end of all things."

26. Ibid., I: 177 (173).

27. Ibid., I: 218 (210–11). "It is true to say that the representative system was just about unknown in Antiquity. In our time, popular passions find it harder to make themselves felt in public affairs; it can be counted on, however, that the representative will always end up conforming to the spirit of the represented which causes the latter's inclinations as well as interests to prevail."

28. Ibid., I: 414 (397).

29. Ibid., II: 67 (475–76). "What one calls the people in the most democratic republics of Antiquity hardly resembles what we mean by the 'people'. In Athens, all the people took part in public affairs; but there were twenty thousand citizens out of more than three hundred and fifty thousand inhabitants; all of the others were slaves and performed most of the functions which belong in our time to the people and even to the middle classes. Athens, with its universal suffrage, was, after all, only an aristocratic republic where all the nobles had

an equal right to govern. It is necessary to consider the struggle between the patricians and plebians in Rome in the same light and to see there only an internal quarrel between the younger and older members of the same family. In effect, all belonged to an aristocracy and possessed its spirit."

30. Ibid., I: 52 (56).
31. Ibid., I: 45–46 (50).
32. Ibid., I: 50–51 (55).

CHAPTER TWO

1. Alexis de Tocqueville, *De la Démocratie en Amerique*, vol. 1, Oeuvres complètes de A. Tocqueville, tome premier (Paris: Gallimard, 1951), 179 (175). All references are to this edition and to its companion volume, *De la Démocratie en Amerique*, vol. II, (Paris: Gallimard, 1951).

2. Ibid., I: 181 (176).
3. Ibid., I: 182 (177–78).
4. This conflict, extremely vehement, fascinated its observers; see, for example, the lengthy comments of Michel Chevalier, *Letters Concerning North America*, 2 vol., (Brussells: 1837). Letters III to VIII of the first volume.
5. Ibid., I: 182 (178).
6. Ibid., I: 183 (179).
7. See also Chapter 21 of the third part of volume II: "*Why Great Revolutions Will Become Rare.*"
8. Ibid., I: 218 (210). "Up to now, with all the nations of the world, the majority has always been composed of those who do not possess property, or those whose property was too limited for them to be able to live in ease without working. Universal suffrage really gives the government of society to the poor."
9. Ibid., I: 205 (198–99).
10. Ibid., I: 244 (234).
11. Ibid., I: 56 (60). See also our earlier discussion in Chapter 1.
12. Alexis de Tocqueville, *L'Ancien Régime et la Révolution*, Vol. I (Paris: Gallimard, 1952) 62–63. This article was published in the introduction to the first volume in the Gallimard edition.
13. See Montesquieu, *The Spirit of the Laws*, XI, 19, and Rousseau, *Social Contract*, III, 15.

14. Cf. Aristotle, *Politics* 1277 a.
15. Ibid., II: 101 (503).
16. Ibid., II: 109 (510).
17. Ibid., II: 109 (509–10).
18. Ibid., II: 320 (609).
19. Ibid., II: 112 (512).
20. Ibid.
21. Ibid., II: 115–16 (515–16).
22. Ibid., II: 122–23 (521–22).
23. Ibid., II: 114 (514).
24. Ibid., II: 304 (674).
25. Ibid., II: 114 (514).
26. See Chapters 5 and 6 of the second part of volume I of *Democracy*.
27. Ibid., I: 169 (164). "Everything is conventional and artificial in such a government."
28. Ibid., I: 325 (311).

CHAPTER THREE

1. Alexis de Tocqueville, *De la Démocratie en Amerique*, vol. II, Oeuvres complètes de A. Tocqueville, tome premier (Paris: Gallimard, 1951) 186 (573). All references are to this edition and to its companion volume, *De la Démocratie en Amerique*, vol. I, (Paris: Gallimard, 1951).
2. Ibid., II: 186 (573).
3. Ibid.
4. Ibid.
5. Ibid., II: 187 (574).
6. Ibid.
7. Ibid., II: 188 (575).
8. Ibid.
9. Ibid., II: 189 (576).
10. Ibid. See also 202 (586): "When most conditions are very unequal and inequality of conditions is permanent, the idea of the superior grows in the imagination of men. . . When, on the contrary, men differ but a little from one another and do not remain consistantly dissimilar, the general idea of the superior grows weaker and less clear. . ."

11. Ibid., II: 187 (574).
12. Ibid., II: 165 (556).
13. Ibid.
14. Ibid.
15. Ibid., II: 166 (556–57).
16. Ibid., 166 (557)
17. Ibid.
18. Ibid.
19. Ibid.
20. Ibid., II: 166–67 (557).
21. Ibid., II: 167 (558).
22. Ibid., II: 199 (584). "In our time this state of misery and dependence in which a part of the industrial population finds itself is an exception and contrary to everything that surrounds it; but, for this very reason there is not something more serious nor something that more merits the particular attention of the legislator. . . ."

23. The *Souvenirs*, principally devoted to the account and analysis of the events of 1848, reveals the hatred that Tocqueville—with all of aristocratic and middle-class France, and with a major part of the French peasantry—feels toward the insurgent workers. In his eyes, they are attempting to attack, not a specific government, but the eternal and necessary order of society itself. Of the June insurrection, he writes: "One must not see there only a brutal and blind effort, but a powerful attempt to escape the necessity of their condition, which had been depicted to them as an illegitimate oppression, and to open a way by blood and iron to an imaginary well-being that had been shown them from afar as a right. It is this mix of avaricious desires and false theories which rendered this insurrection so formidable after having fomented it;" (p. 151 in the Gallimard edition) (Translator's note: See *Recollections: The French Revolution of 1848*, translated by George Lawrence, edited by J.P. Mayer and A.P. Kerr (New York: Doubleday, 1970), 136–37).

CHAPTER FOUR

1. Alexis de Tocqueville, *De la Démocratie en Amerique*, vol. I, Oeuvres complètes de A. Tocqueville, tome premier (Paris: Gallimard, 1951), 265 (254). All references are to this edition and to its companion volume, *De la Démocratie en Amerique*, vol. II, (Paris: Gallimard, 1951).

2. Ibid., I: 266 (255).
3. Ibid.
4. Ibid.
5. Ibid., II: 16 (433).
6. Ibid., II: 17 (434).
7. Ibid.
8. Ibid.
9. Ibid., II: 12 (430).
10. See our discussion on pp. 10–11.
11. Ibid., II: 256 (641). "It is not only trust in the intelligence of certain individuals which weakens in democratic nations; as I said elsewhere, the general idea that any one man whosoever may acquire an intellectual superiority over all others soon fades. As men resemble each other more, the dogma of equality in intelligence little by little insinuates itself into beliefs, and it becomes more difficult for an original mind, in whatever domain, to acquire and exercise a great power over the spirit of a people."
12. Ibid., I: 51 (56).
13. Ibid., I: 51–52; II: 144 (56; 538).
14. Ibid., II: 18 (435).
15. Ibid.
16. Ibid., I: 269 (258).
17. Ibid., I: 267 (256).
18. Ibid., I: 266 (254–55).
19. Ibid., I: 199 (194).
20. Ibid., II: 14 (432).
21. Ibid., II: 18 (436).
22. Ibid., I: 267 (256).
23. Ibid., II: 22 (439).
24. Ibid.
25. Ibid., II: 73 (481).
26. Ibid., II: 74 (482).
27. Ibid., II: 22 (439).
28. Ibid., II: 91 (495).
29. Ibid., II: 92 (496).

CHAPTER FIVE

1. Alexis de Tocqueville, *De la Démocratie en Amerique*, vol. II, Oeuvres complètes de A. Tocqueville, tome premier (Paris: Galli-

mard, 1951) 21 (438). All references are to this edition and to its companion volume, *De la Démocratie en Amerique*, vol. I, (Paris: Gallimard, 1951).

2. Ibid., II: 106 (507).
3. Ibid., II: 172 (562).
4. Ibid., II: 174 (564).
5. Ibid., II: 189 (576–77).
6. Ibid., II: 174 (564).
7. Ibid., II: 172 (562).
8. Ibid., II: 188 (575).
9. Ibid., II: 106 (507).
10. Ibid., I: 110 (109).
11. Ibid.
12. Ibid.
13. Ibid., I: 111 (109–10).
14. Ibid., I: 112 (110–11).
15. Ibid., II: Ch. 6 of part four, 324 (691): "I look in vain myself for an expression that exactly represents the idea I have of it and includes it; the ancient words, "despotism" and "tyranny" are not adequate."
16. Ibid., II: 323 (691). See also Montesquieu, *The Spirit of the Laws*, III, ch. 9.
17. Ibid.
18. Ibid., II: 325 (693).
19. Ibid., II: 326 (694).

CHAPTER SIX

1. Alexis de Tocqueville, *De la Démocratie en Amerique*, vol. II, Oeuvres complètes de A. Tocqueville, tome premier (Paris: Gallimard, 1951) 105 (506). All references are to this edition and to its companion volume, *De la Démocratie en Amerique*, vol. I, (Paris: Gallimard, 1951).

2. Ibid., I: 193 (187).
3. Ibid., II: 134 (530).
4. Ibid., II: 138–39 (534).
5. Ibid., II: 142 (536).
6. Ibid., II: 143 (536).
7. Ibid.

8. Ibid., II: 143 (537)
9. Ibid., I: 421 (403).
10. Ibid.
11. Ibid., I: 420 (402).
12. Ibid., II: 270 (646).
13. See Benjamin Constant, *Of the Spirit of Conquest and Usurpation*, in Constant, *Political Writings* (Cambridge: Cambridge University Press,1988) 43–167.
14. Ibid., II: 284 (657).
15. Ibid.
16. Ibid., II: 284 (657–58).
17. See for example: II: part three, Ch. 18.
18. Ibid., I: 331 (316).
19. See in particular Chapter 13 of the second part of volume II, *"Why the Americans Reveal themselves to be So Anxious Amidst Their Well Being."*
20. Ibid., II: 142–43 (536).
21. Ibid., II: 284 (658).
22. Ibid., II: 144 (537).
23. Ibid., II: 101 (503).
24. Ibid., II: 144 (538).
25. Ibid., II: 302 (673).
26. Ibid., II: 308 (678).
27. Ibid., II: 302 (673).
28. See our discussion in Chapter 2.

CHAPTER SEVEN

1. Alexis de Tocqueville, *De la Démocratie en Amerique*, vol. II, Oeuvres complètes de A. Tocqueville, tome premier (Paris: Gallimard, 1951) 48–49 (461). All references are to this edition and to its companion volume, *De la Démocratie en Amerique*, vol. I, (Paris: Gallimard,1951).
2. Ibid., II: 49 (461–62).
3. Ibid., 49 (462)
4. Ibid.
5. Ibid., II: 252 (629–30).
6. Ibid., I: 215 (208).
7. Ibid., I: 358 (342).

8. Ibid., II: 201 (586).
9. Ibid.
10. Ibid., II: 202 (586).
11. Ibid., II: 203 (587).
12. Ibid., II: 204 (588).
13. Ibid., 204 (589)
14. See our discussion in Chapter 5.
15. Ibid., II: 204 (589).
16. Ibid., II: 203 (587).
17. Ibid., II: 205 (589).
18. Ibid., 205 (589)
19. Ibid.
20. Ibid.
21. Ibid., II: 239 (617).
22. Ibid., II: 248 (626).
23. Ibid., II: 249 (626–27).
24. Ibid., II: 249 (627).
25. Ibid., II: 288, note 2 (660).
26. Ibid., II: 338 (704–05).
27. Ibid., II: 241 (619).
28. See our discussion at the beginning of Chapter 3.
29. For the family, see our discussion earlier in this chapter; for the commune, see: I: 58 (62): "The commune is the sole association so in harmony with nature that where men come together, they form a commune . . . the commune appears to emerge directly from the hands of God."
30. See I: 169 (164): "All is conventional and artificial in such a government. . ."
31. See Pascal, *Three Discourses on the Condition of the Great*, in Pascal, *Thoughts and Minor Works*, (New York: Collier-Harvard Classics, 1910) 382–88.

CHAPTER EIGHT

1. Alexis de Tocqueville, *De la Démocratie en Amerique*, vol. II, Oeuvres complètes de A. Tocqueville, tome premier (Paris: Gallimard, 1951) 206 (590). All references are to this edition and to its companion volume, *De la Démocratie en Amerique*, vol. I, (Paris: Gallimard,1951).

2. Ibid., II: 216 (598). The equality of conditions tends to put *eros* to sleep: "All men who live in democratic times more or less take on the intellectual habits of the industrial and business classes; their mind takes a serious, calculating and empirical turn; they willingly turn from the ideal to direct themselves toward some visible and immediate goal . . . In such a way, equality does not exactly destroy imagination, but it limits it and allows it to fly only close to the ground. No one is less a dreamer than the citizen of a democracy and one hardly finds the types who want to abandon themselves to leisurely and solitary contemplations that ordinarily precede and produce any grand agitations of the heart."

3. Ibid., II: 220 (601).

4. Ibid., II: 219 (601).

5. Ibid., II: 220 (601).

6. Ibid., II: 222 (603).

7. See Henry James, *The Bostonians*, in Henry James, *Novels 1881–1886*, (New York: Library of America, 1985) and, especially, Henry Adams, *The Education of Henry Adams* in *Novels, Mont Saint Michel, The Education*, (New York: Library of America, 1983): "Sometimes, at dinner, one might wait until talk flagged, and then, as mildly as possible, ask one's liveliest neighbor whether she could explain why the American woman was a failure. Without an instant's hesitation, she was sure to answer: 'Because the American man is a failure!' She meant it. . . . Gay or serious, the question never failed to stir feeling. The cleverer the woman, the less she denied the failure. She was bitter at heart about it. She had failed even to hold the family together, and her children ran away like chickens with their first feathers; the family was extinct like chivalry. She had failed not only to create a new society that satisfied her, but even to hold her own in the old society of church or state. . ." (*The Education of Henry Adams*, Chapter 30, 1124–25, in Library of America edition).

8. The term instinct appears on four occasions in the titles of the first volume of *Democracy*, and one meets there numerous equivalents, such as "tendency," or paraphrases containing the same notion.

9. See our earlier discussion in Chapter 2.

10. Ibid., I: 325 (311).

11. Ibid., I: 181 (176). See also our discussion at the beginning of Chapter 2.

12. See our discussion in Chapter 4.

13. See Chapter 4.

14. Ibid., II: 27 (442).
15. Ibid., 27 (442–43)
16. Ibid., 27 (443)
17. Ibid., II: 28 (444).
18. Ibid., II: 29 (444).
19. Ibid., I: 304 (290).
20. Ibid.
21. Ibid., I: 310 (296–97).
22. Ibid.
23. Ibid., I: 311 (297).
24. Ibid.
25. Ibid., I: 306 (292).
26. Ibid., II: 29 (444).
27. Ibid., I: 306 (292).
28. Ibid., I: 312 (299).
29. Ibid., I: 313 (299).
30. Ibid., I: 9 (16).
31. Ibid., I: 304 (291).
32. See our discussion in Chapter 4.
33. Ibid., I: 306 (292–93).
34. See Montesquieu, *Dissertation on the Romans in Matters of Religion.*
35. Ibid., I: 306 (292).
36. Ibid., I: 292 (279).
37. Ibid., I: 31 (36).
38. Ibid., II: 28 (32).
39. Ibid., II: 37 (42).
40. Ibid., I: 42 (46–47).
41. Ibid., I: 40 (45).
42. Ibid., II: 306 (292).
43. Alexis de Tocqueville, *L'Ancien Régime et la Révolution*, Oeuvres complètes, (Paris: Gallimard, 1952) I: 83 (5). All page references are to this edition. Page references in parentheses are to the rather loose translation, bordering on paraphrase, of Stuart Gilbert, *The Old Regime and the French Revolution* (New York: Doubleday Anchor, 1955).
44. Ibid., I: 83 (5).
45. Ibid., I: 84 (6).
46. Ibid., I: 87 (10).
47. Ibid., I: 88 (12).

48. Ibid., I: 89 (12).
49. Ibid.
50. Ibid., I: 204 (151).
51. Ibid.
52. *Democracy in America*, I: 301 (287–88).
53. See *L'Ancien Régime et la Révolution*, I: 204 (151) and *Democracy in America*, II: 11–12 (429–30).
54. *L'Ancien Régime et la Révolution*, I: 89 (12).
55. *Democracy in America*, II: 288 (660–61).
56. *L'Ancien Régime et la Révolution*, I: p. 89 (13).
57. *Democracy in America*, I: 414 (397).
58. Ibid., II: 37–38 (451–52).
59. See our earlier discussion in Chapter 4.
60. *L'Ancien Régime et la Révolution*, I: 170 (111).
61. Ibid.
62. Ibid., I: 171 (112).
63. Ibid.
64. Ibid., I: 173 (114).
65. Ibid., I: 171–72 (113).
66. Ibid., I: 206 (154–55).
67. *Democracy in America*, I: 301 (287).

CHAPTER NINE

1. See *L'Ancien Régime et la Révolution*, I: 95 (19–20).
2. Ibid.
3. Ibid., I: 96 (20).
4. Ibid., I: 235 (192).
5. Ibid., I: 96 (20). See also p. 65: "The effects of the French Revolution are commonly exaggerated." (This is from the conclusion of "*L'État Social et Politique de la France Avant et Depuis 1789*" in the Gallimard edition of *L'Ancien Régime et la Révolution*).
6. See our discussion in Chapter 2.
7. *L'Ancien Régime et la Révolution*, I: 66. (Conclusion of "*L'État Social et Politique de la France Avant et Depuis 1789*").
8. Ibid., I: 266 (224, note 2). See the note on page 92, line 35 of the French edition: "Given that all monarchies became absolute at about the same epoch, it hardly seems likely that this change of constitution belongs to some particular circumstance which was met by

chance in each state at the same moment. One must believe that all these events, similar and contemporaneous, had to be the product of a general cause . . . this general cause was the passage from one social state to another, from feudal inequality to democratic equality. The nobles were already reduced and the people had not yet been raised, the one too low and the other not high enough to encumber the movements of power. We are talking about one hundred and fifty years, which was like a golden age of princes. . ." A.R.R., I, p. 266. (224, note 2)

9. From the uncompleted sequel to *L'Ancien Régime et la Révolution*, vol. I, published as *L'Ancien Régime et la Révolution*, vol. II, 335. (Paris: Gallimard, 1952) (No English language edition will be cited for this volume).

10. *L'Ancien Régime et la Révolution*, I: 105 (30). The very notion of feudality is a political notion: ". . . feudality, although preeminently belonging to political right. . ." (Ibid., I: 275 [236, note 14]).

11. Ibid., I: 100 (23).

12. Ibid., I: 102 (25–26).

13. Ibid., I: 103 (27).

14. Ibid., I: 178 (121).

15. Ibid., I: 180 (124).

16. This is the title of Chapter 12 of the second part of *L'Ancien Régime et la Révolution*.

17. Ibid., I: 185 (130).

18. Ibid., I: 150 (86).

19. Ibid., I: 144 (78).

20. See Chapter 3.

21. Ibid., I: 146 (81).

22. Ibid., I: 150 (85).

23. Ibid., I: 150–51 (86).

24. Ibid., I: 158 (96).

25. Ibid., I: 158 (97). See Chapter 10 of the second part: *"How the Destruction of Political Liberty and the Separation of the Classes Have Caused Almost All the Maladies from which the Ancien Régime Died."*

26. *L'Ancien Régime et la Révolution*, II: 100. "The veritable mother passion of the revolution, the passion of class distinction."

27. Ibid., II: 106–10.

28. *L'Ancien Régime et la Révolution*, I: 173 (115).

29. Ibid., I: 301–2 (273–74, note 48).

30. Ibid., I: 217 (168).

31. Ibid.

32. Ibid., I: 75 (xiv).
33. See our earlier discussion in Chapter 7.
34. Ibid., I: 247 (207–8).
35. *Democracy in America*, II: 103 (505).
36. *L'Ancien Régime et la Révolution*, I: 302. (274–75, note 50)
37. Ibid. See Chapters 8 and 9 of the second part of volume II.
38. *Democracy in America*, II: 128 (526).
39. Ibid.
40. Ibid., II: 128–29 (526–27).
41. Ibid., II: 128 (526). "I think in this matter that they do not often render themselves justice; for one sees sometimes in the United States as elsewhere citizens abandon themselves to the disinterested and unpremeditated impulses which are natural to man. But the Americans hardly confess to yielding to movements of such a kind; they prefer to render honor to their philosophy than to themselves."
42. Ibid., II: 129 (527).
43. *L'Ancien Régime et la Révolution*, I: 176 (119). "The king inspired in them sentiments that none of the most absolute princes who have appeared since in the world could have given rise to. They have become for us almost incomprehensible, so far has the Revolution extirpated them from our hearts to their very roots. They had for him at the same time the tenderness that one has toward a father and the respect that one owes only to God."
44. *Democracy in America*, I: 389 (373). This calculating patriotism of the Americans gives rise to worries in Tocqueville: "I confess that I do not put trust in this calculating patriotism which is based on interest and that interest, in changing its object, can destroy."
45. See the conclusion of Chapter 1.
46. *Democracy in America*, II: 295 (667). "Equality, which renders men independent of one another, causes them to acquire the habit and taste to follow only their will in their particular actions. This complete independence, which is constantly enjoyed with regard to their equals and in the routines of their private lives, disposes them to look askance at all authority, and soon suggests to them the idea and love of political liberty. Men who live in this time walk down a slope which naturally directs them toward free institutions. Take anyone by chance: go back, if it is possible, to his primitive instincts. You will discover that, among different governments, the one that he imagines first and prizes the most is the government where he elects the leader and controls his actions."

47. Ibid. "In effect, equality produces two tendencies: one leads men directly to independence and can push them all suddenly to the point of anarchy; the other leads them by a longer path, more stealthy but more sure, toward servitude."

48. *L'Ancien Régime et la Révolution*, I: 72 (X–XI); " . . . this first period of '89, where the love of equality and that of liberty shared their [the French] heart; where they wanted to found not only democratic institutions but free ones; not only to destroy privileges but to recognize and consecrate new rights; a time of youth, enthusiasm, pride, generous and sincere passions, which, despite its errors, men eternally retain in their memory, and which, for a long time still, would disturb the sleep of those who would want to corrupt and subject them."; and also "Moment of a moral grandeur without equal in History," *L'Ancien Régime et la Révolution*, II: 131.

49. Letter of A. Gobineau to A. de Tocqueville, November 29, 1856, in *Correspondance d'Alexis de Tocqueville et d'Arthur de Gobineau*, Oeuvres Complètes, (Paris: Gallimard, 1959) tome IX, 273–74. "Permit me to ask you what you find to admire in the members of the Constituent Assembly of 1789? They originated none of the ideas which are commonly attributed to them, and you have put your finger exactly on this. They only precipitated the ruin of what could have made resistance to the full flowering of these ideas, of which surely you do not approve in themselves. . . Why then do you sympathize with these persons? They originated nothing, they showed no guidance in anything, they had foreseen nothing, they engaged in demagoguery, and their actions were limited to opening a door that they wanted left closed, at least, I am willing to grant, in the case of some of them. But as they decried tyranny when there was none, as you amply demonstrate, as they used clubs to kill flies, and as they rushed to throw all aside and did very badly what had been done tranquilly for centuries, I do not see any reason to interest myself in them. There is something, moreover, I maintain, which is rather vile in this assembly which had applauded the first instances of violence, in this drunken comedy of the taking of the Bastille, in these first massacres, in these burnings of chateaus, thinking none of that would ever affect them and simply because they had never foreseen that they were severing the head from their own torso, do you think that one could characterize the evil that they did as a generous error? Why generous?"

50. *Democracy in America*, II: 337–38 (704).